T0003800

WHY DOGS EAT POOP

Gross but True Things You Never Knew About Animals

Francesca Gould
&
David Haviland

ILLUSTRATED BY
JP Coovert

G. P. Putnam's Sons
An Imprint of Penguin Group (USA) Inc.

Also by Francesca Gould

Why You Shouldn't Eat Your Boogers:

Gross but True Things You Don't Want to Know
About Your Body

For Mum

G. P. PUTNAM'S SONS
An imprint of Penguin Young Readers Group
Published by The Penguin Group
Penguin Group (USA) Inc., 375 Hudson Street, New York, NY 10014, USA

USA | Canada | UK | Ireland | Australia | New Zealand | India | South Africa | China
Penguin Books Ltd, Registered Offices: 80 Strand, London WC2R 0RL, England
For more information about the Penguin Group, visit penguin.com

Text copyright © 2010 by Francesca Gould and David Haviland.
Originally published in 2010 by Piatkus UK as *Self-Harming Parrots and Exploding Toads*.
First American edition 2010, Tarcher/Penguin.
Abridgement copyright © 2013 Penguin Group (USA) Inc.
Illustrations copyright © 2013 by JP Coovert.
All rights reserved. No part of this book may be reproduced, scanned or distributed in any
printed or electronic form without permission in writing from the publisher. G. P. Putnam's Sons,
Reg. U.S. Pat. & Tm. Off. Please do not participate in or encourage piracy of copyrighted
materials in violation of the author's rights. Purchase only authorized editions.

Library of Congress Cataloging-in-Publication Data
Gould, Francesca.
Why dogs eat poop : gross but true things you never knew about animals / Francesca Gould and
David Haviland ; illustrated by J. P. Coovert.
pages cm
Audience: 8–12.
Audience: Grade 4 to 6.
1. Animals—Miscellanea—Juvenile literature. 2. Animal behavior—Juvenile literature. I. Haviland,
David. II. Coovert, J. P., illustrator. III. Title. QL50.G693 2013 591.5—dc23 2012051012

Published simultaneously in Canada. Printed in the United States of America.
ISBN 978-0-399-16530-6
1 3 5 7 9 10 8 6 4 2

Design by Marikka Tamura. Text set in Diverda Serif.
The publisher does not have any control over and does not assume any responsibility
for author or third-party websites or their content.

Contents

1
Amazing Animals

Which Octopus
Is an Expert Impressionist ?

There's a species of octopus that can mimic an incredible range of other sea life. It's a small, brown-and-white-mottled mollusk called the mimic octopus, which is about 2 feet (61 cm) long, and found in waters around Indonesia. It can change its color and shape to resemble much of the local fauna. Many types of octopus can change color, and some are even believed to be able to mimic one other species, but the mimic octopus is the first known animal of any kind that can morph into a number of different physical impersonations in this way.

It can mimic at least 15 other species, including sea snakes, lionfish, flatfish, sole fish, brittle stars, giant crabs, sea stars, stingrays, flounders, jellyfish, sea anemones, and mantis shrimps. For example, it impersonates a sea snake by stuffing seven of its arms into a hole and waving the remaining one in the water. It impersonates lionfish by hovering above the ocean floor with its arms spread out, trailing from its body, just like the lionfish's poisonous fins. Its impression of a sole consists of building up speed through jet propulsion and drawing its arms in so that its body forms a flat wedge that undulates just like the flat body of a sole.

This talent seems to be useful in two particular ways. First, the mimic octopus uses this skill to get closer to its prey. For example, it will pretend to be a female crab to get closer to an amorous male crab, which it will then grab and eat. It also uses mimicry to scare off its predators. Most of the species it mimics are poisonous, and the octopus can tailor its impressions to the intended audience, ensuring that it mimics the creature that will be most likely to discourage or scare off the predator. For example, when approached by a damselfish, a mimic octopus will suddenly appear to turn into a banded sea snake, which is a known predator of damselfish.

If You Cut an Earthworm in Half, Do You End Up with Two Worms?

No. If you cut an earthworm in half, all you will usually end up with is two halves of a dead worm. Like most creatures, an earthworm cut in half will probably die. The only way it might survive is if the cut is made behind the thickest part of the worm, which is called the saddle, where all its major organs are found. If all these organs are retained, the worm may survive, but it will still just be one worm.

There is one type of worm, though, that will form two new worms if cut in half. A planarian is a flatworm that is found in many parts of the world, in salt water and fresh water and on land. Amazingly, a planarian can be cut across its width or its length, and both halves will regenerate as a living worm. This is

> a planarian worm can be **cut across** its width or its length, and both **halves** will **regenerate** as a living worm

possible because flatworms have very simple body structures, with none of the complex organs that an earthworm requires to survive.

Which Bird Drinks Blood?

The Galápagos Islands are very dry, with a lack of fresh water. Birds need water in their diet, so the vampire finch has found a number of ways to quench its thirst. First, it drinks nectar from the flowers of the Galápagos prickly pear. Second, it steals eggs, rolling them from their nests and smashing them to drink the nourishing yolk inside.

The vampire finch's third method is even more extraordinary: it drinks the blood of other birds, usually masked boobies and red-footed boobies. It does this by pecking the skin in front of the bird's tail until it bleeds. Surprisingly, the boobies don't seem to mind being pecked and offer little resistance. Some believe that this behavior may have evolved from an earlier mutually beneficial habit of picking parasites from the boobies' skin. Over time, the finches may have inadvertently begun to draw blood and continued the practice as the nutritious blood became a key source of protein and liquid.

There is another type of bird, the oxpecker, that does something similar. Oxpeckers are

oxpeckers reopen wounds and feed on the other animals' blood

found in Africa and feed exclusively on the backs and necks of large mammals, including cattle, rhinos, buffalo, antelopes, impalas, and giraffes. It used to be thought that oxpeckers enjoyed a mutually beneficial relationship with their hosts: the theory was that the oxpeckers cleaned the large mammals' skin by pecking away ticks, botfly larvae, and other parasites, often from hard-to-reach spots such as inside the animals' nostrils or ears.

However, recent research suggests that, like vampire finches, oxpeckers may simply be parasites that perhaps once helped clean their hosts but now subsist chiefly by reopening wounds and feeding on the animals' blood. Oxpeckers do remove some ticks and larvae from their hosts, yet evidence indicates that they may not remove enough of them to make any meaningful difference.

Which Creature Builds Itself a Refrigerator

Many mammals that live in cold climates are forced to hibernate in winter because a lack of available food requires them to conserve as much heat and energy as possible. But beavers have an amazing way of surviving the winter without having to sleep through it and miss out on all the fun. They build themselves an underwater refrigerated pantry, which provides them with a constant supply of fresh, nutritious food throughout the winter, even when the woods around them are barren and covered with snow.

When setting up home for the first time, a pair of beavers will choose a valley with a small stream running through it and build a dam. Beavers are big, powerful creatures that can grow to 4 feet (1.2 m) in length and have enormous, sharp teeth. With these, they cut down trees and drag them into place on the streambed. This construction is supported with rocks and then plastered with mud on the upstream side. On the downstream side, more tree trunks are laid lengthwise up against the dam wall to provide support against the increasing weight of the water. Gradually, the lake behind the dam begins to swell, so the beavers respond by lengthening the dam. As this process continues, they may use up all the nearby trees and have to travel long distances to find more. Beavers sometimes even build canals to transport wood down to their dam. A pair of beavers may maintain their dam for years, with some dams eventually becoming more than 100 yards (91.4 m) long.

Once the dam is built, the beavers start work on their underground lodge, where they will spend the winter. This will either be on the edge of the lake or preferably on an island for added security. The beavers build a tunnel that opens on the surface of the island and leads down to a second, underwater entrance. They cover the land entrance with rocks, branches, and mud and then excavate the inside of the mound, creating a large, hollow chamber. They are now extremely safe since their underground chamber is secure from above and they can slip into the water unseen.

When autumn comes, the beavers start to fill their pantry for the winter. They collect leafy branches and submerge them in the lake, where the near-freezing water will keep them fresh and green. As the temperature drops, the roof of the beavers' lodge freezes solid, making it practically impenetrable, and their food stays fresh safely at the bottom of the lake.

Which Insects Are
Used for Cleaning Museums **?**

This sounds like a mistake. Surely you clean museums *of* insects, not *with* them? Nonetheless, there is a type of beetle that museum curators find extremely useful. The dermestid beetle eats dead skin, flesh, and hair, and one single beetle can strip the skin off a dead animal in just a few hours, leaving a perfect, pristine skeleton. Natural history museums use the amazing nibblers to clean animal bones that are to be used as exhibits. They are used by taxidermists for similar purposes.

Dermestid beetles can also be used by the police to help calculate how long a body has been dead, in a science called forensic entomology. Investigators generally focus on flies and maggots, which are usually

> **one single beetle** can strip the skin off a **dead animal** in **just a few hours,** leaving a perfect, **pristine skeleton**

the first on the scene; but if a body has been left to decay for some time, the presence of beetles is also a useful indicator. Dermestid beetles will appear during the final stages of decomposition to feed on the dried skin, tendon, and bone left behind by the earlier scavengers. Dermestids usually appear around five to 11 days after death.

In addition to preying on the dead, dermestids have a tendency to annoy the living. They are omnivores that love to eat grain, and they cause millions of dollars' worth of crop damage every year, making them a major irritation for farmers. They can also cause havoc in your home if you're unlucky enough to become infested. Let a dermestid beetle into your home, and it will munch your carpet right down to the bare floorboards.

Which Reptile Solves Crimes?

Snapping turtles, freshwater turtles that are found in the Americas, mainly like to eat rotting meat, and they have a particular talent for sniffing out dead carcasses in the water. This ability has led police to use snapping turtles to help them find human corpses underwater. According to reports, the police simply tie a line to the turtle, and it leads them straight to the body. There are two species: the enormous alligator snapping turtle, which can weigh over 200 pounds (about 90 kg), and the common snapping turtle, which is smaller, rarely weighing more than 60 pounds (27 kg). Both species have large heads, which cannot be withdrawn into their small shells. They have very strong jaws and mobile necks, and will bite aggressively if threatened.

Do Birds Have Accents

A bird's ability to sing is partly inherited and partly taught by its parents. Scientists have demonstrated this by conducting tests on chaffinch chicks. If the chicks are reared in silence, they will still attempt to sing, but their calls will be only barely recognizable as a chaffinch call. They have to hear their parents sing before they are able to produce the full range and subtleties of the usual chaffinch song.

Since these songs are passed down through the generations, we might therefore imagine that birds in different regions would develop distinctions, regional accents. And this turns out to be true. Experts can recognize the different accents of chaffinches from northern England compared with those from the south.

In the nineteenth century, Australian settlers imported many plant and animal species from Europe to make them feel more at home in their strange new land. These included a range of songbirds such as blackbirds, which were not indigenous to Australia. Today, little more than a century later, the descendants of those blackbirds have developed a distinctive Australian accent.

blackbirds have developed a distinctive Australian accent

What Is a Remote-Control Cockroach?

Cockroaches may be unpleasant, but they are also remarkable creatures, and we can learn a great deal from them. Scientists love cockroaches because they're great for experimenting on. The nerve cells in their brains are quite similar to ours, and they also grow tumors that are like those of humans. As a result, scientists use cockroaches to study cancer, heart disease, and even the inner workings of the brain.

In one fascinating experiment, scientists at the University of Tokyo found that they could remove a cockroach's wings, insert tiny electrodes into its antennae, and use these to "drive" it via remote control, making it stop, go, and turn left and right. To power the electrodes, the cockroaches were also fitted with tiny backpacks containing batteries.

Now, this experiment may sound frivolous, but it could have valuable applications. Scientists are looking into the possibility of using remote-

control cockroaches in res-
cue work. With tiny cameras
on their backs, cockroaches
could be very useful in ex-
ploring collapsed buildings
and other dangerous, inac-
cessible locations.

with tiny cameras on their backs, cockroaches could be very useful

In fact, cockroaches are not the only creatures to have been experimented on in this way. In recent years, scientists have carried out similar tests on remote-control rats, pigeons, and sharks. In theory, remote-control animals such as these could have numerous useful applications, including military surveillance, clearing land mines, or mapping underground areas. The advantage of using real animals in this way rather than building robots is that these animals can already deal with problems such as walking, turning, climbing, and avoiding obstacles, which turn out to be very difficult for real robots to accomplish, at least at present.

Who Was the Last Known
Speaker of the Ature Language ?

The language of the Atures people of Venezuela died out during the nineteenth century. The German explorer and geographer Alexander von Humboldt was lucky enough to meet the very last speaker of this language while trekking through the Venezuelan jungle. During his expedition, von Humboldt made many fascinating discoveries, including the electric eel, the Brazil nut, and a previously undiscovered ocean current off the west coast of South America. Still, he had not managed to discover a single word of the Ature language.

Then, while visiting the neighboring tribe of Maypures, he finally made a breakthrough. He was led by torchlight through the remote village to the cage of a talking parrot. The Maypures explained that this bird had been captured long ago, from the Atures people, who were now extinct. The bird began to speak, and von Humboldt recorded the 40 words that the parrot knew, the only remaining vocabulary of what had once been an entire language.

Which Amphibian Can Survive Being Frozen ?

Alaska and Canada are home to several hardy frog species that somehow have to survive the icy winter. The solution found by two of them, wood frogs and chorus frogs, is that their bodies can be frozen almost solid, and they still survive. In this state of

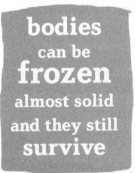

hibernation, more than two-thirds of the water in the frog's body turns to ice, and its heart stops. If you were to pick one up and cut it with a knife, it wouldn't bleed. Nonetheless, it is still alive.

In most animals, freezing temperatures are dangerous because ice crystals can form in their blood vessels and rupture the soft walls. Freezing can also damage skin and stop blood flow to parts of the body that are far from the heart, which can lead to frostbite. However, these amazing frogs have found a way of surviving these threats. When ice starts to form on their bodies, they begin producing extra glucose (sugar in the blood) in their livers, and this functions as antifreeze, flowing into their bodies' cells and preventing them from being damaged through freezing. Simultaneously, water drains out of the cells and into the spaces between them. This water will freeze, but it will not harm the bodies' organs. Having survived the winter, the frogs will then begin to thaw as the temperature rises in spring.

There are a number of other creatures that can survive subzero temperatures. The Siberian salamander can also survive in temperatures as low as minus 58° F (minus 50° C). It too produces a kind of chemical antifreeze before it hibernates, which protects its cells from rupturing. The Arctic woolly bear caterpillar can survive being frozen solid for 10 months in the tundra, where temperatures drop that low as well. The Arctic ground squirrel also allows its body temperature to drop below freezing—and survives. As yet, scientists haven't found an antifreeze in the squirrels like that of the wood frogs, so it's still unclear how this squirrel manages to survive the cold.

Scorpions are normally found only in warm countries, but they can withstand freezing for several weeks and can survive being underwater for two days. Their appetite is so small that some can go without any food or water for an astonishing 12 months. To top it all off, some scorpions can live for as long as 30 years.

Which Bird Can Sew?

A number of birds have developed sewing skills to construct their nests. Examples include three birds of the warbler family: the golden-headed cisticola in Australia, the evergreen forest warbler in Africa, and the aptly named tailorbird of India.

Each of these birds has a long, thin beak, which it uses like a needle. For thread, they use spiders' silk, cotton from seeds, and fibers from the bark of trees.

To sew, the bird selects two leaves that are still growing. Holding their edges together, with a fiber in its beak, it makes a hole through both leaves and threads the fiber through. It twists both ends of this thread, locking the stitch in place. It takes about six of these stitches to turn a pair of leaves into a cup, which can then be filled with grass and used as a nest.

There are other birds that practice an even more difficult craft: weaving. In South America, orioles, oropendolas, and caciques all weave their nests. In Arica, there are a number of sparrow species that weave. They do so by tearing a fibrous strip from a leaf and threading it alternately over and under other strips. This is a difficult business, requiring some degree of forward planning and judgment since the bird has to decide how taut each strip should be, how much each wall of the planned structure should curve, and what the final shape should be. Some of the nests built in this way are extremely neat and precise.

How Do Catfish Predict Earthquakes ?

There is a Japanese myth about a giant catfish, Namazu, who lives in the mud under the string of islands that make up the country of Japan. The god Kashima usually contains him, but when he drops his guard, Namuza shakes his powerful tail and causes earthquakes. The origin of the myth may have been the actual behavior of the fish.

Catfish have the most finely tuned senses of any creature. They have more taste buds than any other animals—in fact, their entire bodies are covered in them. Their senses of smell, hearing, and touch are also amazingly powerful.

A catfish can also pick up ultra-low-frequency sound using its lateral line, which is a line of small pores along the fish's side. These pores contain tiny hairlike projections that are extremely sensitive to vibrations, and people say that the fish become more active in the days leading up to an earthquake.

There is also evidence that some other animals can sense earthquakes. After the Indian Ocean tsunami in December 2004, there were numerous reports of strange animal behavior. At the Yala National Park in Sri Lanka, where 60 humans 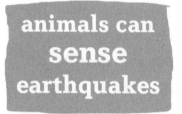 died, not one animal was killed. On India's Cuddalore coast, where thousands of people died, the local goats, buffalo, and other animals seemed to have escaped largely unharmed. There were various anecdotal reports of animals running for higher ground and abandoning their usual territories in the days leading up to the tsunami.

How could the animals have sensed that an earthquake was coming? One possible explanation is that the animals may have sensed the energy changes deep within the earth. In 1998, scientists in Japan tested this theory by observing laboratory animals' behavior while blocks of granite were crushed by machines nearby. As the pressure on the blocks grew, the animals visibly became more anxious.

Which Spider Builds Its Home Underwater?

There is an amazing spider that is able to spend its life underwater even though, like all spiders, it cannot breathe in water. So how does it do it? The answer is that it builds itself an airtight underwater capsule, which it fills with oxygen and lives inside. It is known as the water spider, or diving bell spider.

The first stage is to weave a tight web underwater, between two plant stems. The spider manages to stay submerged by breathing the bubbles of air that get trapped in the hairs of its abdomen, and it frequently returns to the surface. Once the web is complete, the spider surfaces once more to capture a large bubble of air between its two hind legs. It swims back down with its other six legs (which is hard work since the bubble of air is buoyant) and traps the big bubble of air as well as any other smaller bubbles trapped on its abdomen under the web. It repeats this step many more times, frequently adding more threads to support and expand the web until this underwater air chamber is about the size of an acorn, making it considerably bigger than the spider itself, which is just half an inch (13 mm) long. When it needs more oxygen, the spider simply swims to the surface and brings down another bubble.

From this chamber, the spider darts out at unsuspecting prey, which may include passing tadpoles, small fish, and other pond life. Sometimes it eats insects that have been unlucky enough to fall in the water. It swims to the surface to grab them and then drags them back to its chamber.

The water spider needs to return to its bubble to eat because, like all spiders, it doesn't eat its prey whole. It inserts digestive fluids from its salivary glands into its prey, waits for the fluids to turn the insides of the prey into liquid, and then drinks that liquid. And the spider doesn't just hunt underwater. It lives in this diving bell, even mating there and bringing up its young!

Can Ants Be Farmers?

The short answer is yes. Just as human farmers can have dairy farms, ants have aphid farms.

Aphids are small, soft-bodied insects that feed on the sugary sap of plants. They mainly need the nitrogen in the sap, and it takes a great deal of sap for them to get enough. This leads to lots of liquid waste, which grows out of their bodies in big sugary drops of honeydew. Honeydew may be a waste product for aphids, but ants prize it very highly.

When ants find a large group of aphids, they will milk them for their honeydew, like human farmers milking cows. The ants will tend and protect a herd of aphids in much the same way as a farmer looks after his cattle. Ants will build a shelter of leaves and soil to shield the aphids from rain or fence them in. They herd the aphids back to the ant colony at night and may then take them to a new spot to graze the next day, even selecting plants that will lead to higher production of honeydew. The ants' effort is well rewarded because the aphids can produce more than their own weight in honeydew in a single hour. Some aphid species even produce three times as much honeydew if regularly milked, just like cows.

Ants are not just aphid farmers. There are also more than 200 species of ants that grow their own food. Leaf-cutter ants do not eat the leaves they collect—instead, they grow fungus gardens on the leaves and eat the fungi. These ants tend their gardens carefully, keeping them well fertilized and free of bacteria, pests, and mold. Amazingly, the fungi that these ants grow are found nowhere else on earth.

What Animal Waste Is Used in Perfume for Humans?

Civets are mammals found in the tropical regions of Africa and Asia. They look like a cross between a cat and a mongoose, with dark, mottled fur. Civets are tree dwellers whose diet consists of fruit, insects, worms, and some small vertebrates such as squirrels, rats, and birds.

But *civet* is also the name given to the musk produced by a gland that is found on the animal's rear end. Civets smear this oil on their homes and on rocks and branches in their territory as a sign of ownership to warn off rivals. Civet, in this sense, is a thick, oily substance with such a powerful, unpleasant smell that the tiniest whiff of it can actually make a person physically sick. Many other small mammals, including cats, badgers, skunks, and weasels, use similar secretions to mark their territory.

the **tiniest** whiff of **musk** can actually make a person physically **sick**

Because civet oil is so powerful and long-lasting, it became highly prized by perfumers. Although it smells terrible on its own, when civet oil is combined with other scents, it heightens their smell, making it stronger. It also makes them release their scent extremely slowly, so that the perfume smell lasts a long time.

You'll be happy to know that today, most perfume manufacturers use man-made oil rather than civet oil.

2
Peculiar Parents

Which Amphibian Feeds Her Own Skin to Her Young ?

Caecilians look like worms and live in the ground, but they are actually amphibians. They are found in the tropical regions of Asia, Africa, and South America; there are at least 170 species of them and probably many more. One of these species, *Boulengerula taitanus*, has an extraordinary way of feeding her young. When she has laid her cluster of eggs, she then curls her long body around them protectively. Once they hatch, the young start to bite her, tearing off strips of her skin. She allows this to happen until they have eaten the entire outer layer of her body. This takes place in a frenzy, which lasts about seven minutes. The family will then rest for three days, giving the mother time to grow a new layer of skin, before they dig in again.

You might think that this would hurt or damage the mother, but actually it seems to do her no harm. This is because she grows a new outer layer of skin before giving birth, making her twice as thick as before, for just this purpose. Like mammals' milk, this new skin is an excellent source of nutrients for the growing larvae. This practice is known as dermatotrophy, and the caecilian is the only amphibian known to practice it.

There is another species of caecilian that has a similarly bizarre way of feeding her young. In this species, the mother retains her eggs within her oviduct—the tube through which the egg passes— for much longer, so that the larvae hatch while still inside her. These larvae also feast on the mother's body. But rather than gnaw on her external skin, they eat the interior lining of her oviduct. In this species, the larvae can remain within their mother, cannibalizing her in this bizarre way, for up to 11 months.

Why Do Birds of Prey Encourage Their Young to Kill One Another?

As unpleasant as it may sound, many birds of prey, such as the harpy eagle and the bald eagle, will usually lay two eggs and then encourage one of the hatchlings to kill and eat the other. The parents will usually give the elder sibling most of the food and allow it to bully and harass the younger one until it dies. The favorite now eats his younger sibling, which means that the energy and nutrition that the parents invested in the second hatchling still benefit their family. The reason for this shocking approach to parenting seems to be that the birds' best chance of raising healthy offspring is to focus all their resources and energy on one chick, and so the second egg is little more than an insurance policy, in case the first egg doesn't hatch or gets destroyed in some way.

when the second egg is laid, the first is pushed out of the nest and rarely survives

The macaroni penguin does something slightly different. It also lays two eggs, but the second egg it lays is favored. The first egg is usually less than two-thirds the size of the second egg. About four days later, when the second egg is laid, the first is pushed out of the nest and rarely survives.

One reason the first egg may be so frail is that the penguins' eggs are in most danger of getting eaten or destroyed at the start of the breeding season, when the colony is just getting established. During this time, the adults are busy fighting, and birds steal many of the eggs. Another theory is that the development of the first egg is stunted because it begins while the mother is migrating from the ocean to the land. Therefore, the penguins have evolved a tendency to favor the second egg, which is more likely to result in a healthy offspring.

Which Creature Kills Its Siblings While Still in the Womb?

The sand tiger shark is a fierce-looking predator that is found in coastal waters all over the world. Despite its appearance and large size—it can grow to a length of more than 10 feet (3 m)—it is not regarded as being particularly aggressive, although there have been some reported attacks on humans.

This shark has a fascinating and gruesome way of reproducing. It has two wombs, which each contain a number of fertilized eggs. The baby sharks hatch while still inside their mother's womb, and the first ones to hatch quickly eat all the unhatched eggs. They then start to hunt down and kill one another until just two survivors remain, one in each womb.

the **first baby** to hatch quickly **eats** all the **unhatched eggs**

Usually the first shark to hatch in each womb will be the one to survive since it had a significant head start on its siblings. One advantage of having two wombs is that the shark will usually end up producing two healthy, well-fed offspring. To provide further nourishment, the mother will continue to produce eggs for the two survivors to eat.

The offspring remain inside their mother for an astonishing two years, until they reach around 3 feet (1 m) long and are quite capable of fending for themselves. This is important because as soon as they are born, they will have to hunt and feed and defend themselves independently. Amazingly, there are reports of scientists touching the bellies of heavily pregnant sand tiger sharks and feeling the outline of the sharp, fully developed teeth of the young sharks still inside her womb!

Which Amphibian Emerges from Its Mother's Back

The Surinam toad is found in tropical South America and is a pretty weird creature, even for a toad. It is usually about 4 to 5 inches (10 to 12 cm) long, and its body is extremely flat, as if it has been stepped on. When two of these toads want to mate, they dance together in the water, somersaulting gracefully around each other. The female ejects her eggs and the male simultaneously releases his sperm so that the eggs are immediately fertilized in the water. He then spreads the toes of one foot and, using this foot like a spatula, collects the eggs and spreads them over the female's back. The pair continue to dance together, and each time they somersault, he spreads more eggs onto her back. Gradually, the skin of the female's back starts to swell up, trapping the eggs inside. Within a day or so, the skin will have regrown over the eggs, forming a strange-looking honeycomb.

The eggs now remain trapped within the female's skin, even after they hatch into tadpoles. All the while, they are absorbing nutrients from their mother and continuing to grow. Soon, you can actually see the tadpoles wriggling underneath her skin. Twenty-four days after fertilization,

> you can actually see the tadpoles wriggling underneath her skin

they break through the skin of their mother's back and swim off on their own, not as tadpoles, but as fully developed miniature toads, each less than 1 inch (2.5 cm) long.

Which Insect Drinks the Blood of Its Own Young?

A type of ant recently discovered in Madagascar has an unusual and gruesome way of feeding. The Dracula ant, which is a member of the *Adetomyrma* genus, sucks the blood of its own larvae. It cuts holes into the larvae's body and feeds on the blood that oozes out. The larvae do survive being cannibalized in this way, but they are left marked and scarred.

Which Male Frog Likes to Give His Young a Leg Up in Life?

Male European midwife toads take an active and ingenious role in the reproductive process. The male will usually live near a pond, in a damp hole in the ground. When he is ready to mate, he will make a series of short, peeping calls in the hope that a female will respond. If a female does come to visit him, he holds her with his forelegs while she begins to produce eggs in strings several dozen long that rest on her thighs. The male now crouches on all fours and releases sperm onto the eggs. Then, after about 15 minutes, he lifts his legs and ties the eggs onto his thighs with the strings. Once he has collected them all, the female leaves, and he now takes care of the eggs.

The male toad carries the eggs around with him, strapped to his thighs, for a number of weeks. If the weather is dry, he will take the eggs down to the pond for a dip so that they stay moist. When it is time for the tadpoles to emerge, he goes down to the pond at night and lowers his hind legs into the

the **male** toad **carries** the **eggs** **strapped** to his **thighs**

water. Over a couple of hours, the tadpoles will free themselves and swim off, leaving their devoted father behind.

Why Do Penduline Tits Hide Their Eggs?

Penduline tits are small, pretty birds that can reach around 4.5 inches (11 cm) in length and are found in most parts of eastern and southern Europe. The male weaves an impressive, baglike nest, which hangs from a tree, usually over the water. It is this pendulous nest that gives the birds their name. Once the nest is completed, the male calls to nearby females, hoping to persuade them to mate. The females will tour the various local nests, assessing their size and quality. In general, the female will select the biggest nest available. She indicates her choice by landing on the nest, carrying a beakful of wool, which will form the lining.

Once she has moved in, the female takes over the construction work herself. She brings in more lining and digs an entrance tube pointing downward. Once she's happy with her new home, she mates with the male and begins to lay her eggs. This is when things start to get really interesting.

Both the male and female want to leave the nest as soon as the eggs have been laid so that they can go start a second family. But they will leave only if they know that the eggs in this first nest will be looked after—both of them have already invested too much in this brood to just let the eggs die. Therefore, each tries to leave the incubation and raising of the offspring to the other.

> both the **male** and **female** want to leave the nest as soon as the **eggs** have been laid

They do this using some sneaky tactics. Usually, a clutch consists of six eggs. As a result, once a male notices that his partner has laid six eggs, he will leave at the first opportunity. That way, she will be forced to stay and look after the eggs while he can build another nest and raise another family.

To counter this risk, the female may start to hide her eggs. After laying two of them, she may bring in more nest lining and cover them up. The male doesn't seem to be able to remember how many eggs have been laid, so as long as they are out of sight, he is unaware of them. He will continue to mate with her while she continues to lay—and hide—the eggs. Eventually, she will have her six eggs, at which point she removes the lining exposing the eggs and takes off. When the unwitting male returns to the nest, he has no choice but to raise his brood single-handed while the female goes off and finds another partner.

How Do Birds Decide Which of Their Young to Feed

When a bird parent arrives back at its nest, it may find a number of chicks pleading to be fed. They open their beaks as wide as they can, displaying their bright red gapes (the inside of their mouths), while the parent has to decide which hungry mouth gets the food. But how does it decide?

It seems that the color of the chick's gape is crucial. Birds are more likely to feed the chicks that have the brightest, reddest gape. There are a number of possible explanations for this. In some birds, such as young linnets, the red color of the gapes comes from the blood vessels in the throat. If, however, the chick has already been fed, some of its blood will be diverted to its stomach to digest the food, leaving the gape a duller red. Therefore, a brighter gape indicates which chick has not yet been fed.

Another theory is that the parent will feed the bird with the brightest gape because this is a good indication of the bird's health. A red gape indicates that the bird has a strong immune system. According to this argument, the parent's choice serves to favor the strongest chicks, which have the best chance of living.

Some birds have evolved to take advantage of this tendency. Cuckoos lay their eggs in the nests of other birds, including dunnocks, meadow pipits, and Eurasian reed warblers. When the cuckoo chicks hatch, these interlopers will try to push the host's own chicks out of the nest and beg for food from the parent bird, seemingly using their exceptionally bright red gapes to win favor.

One type of cuckoo, the Hodgson's hawk-cuckoo, has even evolved gape-colored patches under its wings. The parent birds of the nests it invades place food into one of these patches, as if they are fooled into thinking it's the mouth of one of their young.

Why Does One Type of Lizard Lay Its Eggs Inside a Termite Nest

Reptiles lay delicate, fragile eggs that are very sensitive to temperature and moisture. In too dry an environment, the egg's shell would allow too much moisture to escape, drying out the contents and killing the embryo. If the temperature is too hot or cold, the embryo will also die. Consequently, finding the ideal spot to lay the egg is a crucial part of the reptile's reproductive process.

A number of species of monitor lizard have found a clever place to lay their eggs: in the center of a termite nest. Termite nests are one of the natural world's most astounding constructions. They are built in such a way that the temperature and humidity inside the nest remain perfectly constant. There are shafts and chimneys to create updrafts within the nest, spreading the hot air generated by the termites working in the basements of the nest. The termites manage the humidity carefully, too, bringing water up if the atmosphere inside the nest becomes too dry or hot.

This well-maintained environment is the perfect place for the monitor lizard to lay her eggs. She will rip a hole in the nest with her powerful claws and deposit her eggs in the very center of the nest. Then she simply leaves. The termites immediately begin rebuilding the nest because a change in temperature can be disastrous for their own young. Within hours, the broken walls will have been repaired and the nest's temperature and humidity restored to proper levels. The termites seem oblivious to the lizard's eggs sitting in the heart of their nest.

After a few months, the eggs hatch and the young monitor lizards struggle free of their shells. However, they are too big to climb out of the termites' tunnels, so they either have to dig their way out or wait for their mother to come and break the nest open again.

Which Animals Make the Best Parents?

We have now heard many stories of cruel and lazy animal parenthood, but what about the heroes of animal parenthood? Which parent offers the most caring, nurturing environment for its young? Is it the male emperor penguin, which spends the winter in the frozen Antarctic, huddled with his brothers, each balancing a single, precious egg on the top of his feet? Or is it perhaps the female Australian social spider, which makes the ultimate sacrifice, allowing her young to feast on her body, killing her in the process?

> one **spider** allows her young to **feast on her body**, killing her in the process

Well, perhaps one way of measuring a parent's performance is to see how long the family unit stays together. If the young remain by their parents' side for a long time, it's a fair bet that they're being well looked after. According to this criterion, the clear winner is the killer whale, which is also called an orca. Killer whales form the most stable family groups of all mammals. Astonishingly, after 25 years of intensive research, watching killer whales in the coastal waters of the northeastern Pacific Ocean, researchers have not observed one single incidence of a killer whale ever leaving its mother. As far as we know, every killer whale stays with its family group for its entire life.

How Do Stick Insects Get Ants to Incubate Their Eggs

Stick insects like to keep things simple. Often, female stick insects don't even bother involving the male in the business of reproduction. Instead, a female will simply produce eggs all by herself. Then, rather than care for the eggs, the stick insect mother simply lets them drop to the ground. Yet the species endures, thanks to a number of cunningly designed evolutionary traits.

rather than **care for** the eggs, the stick insect **mother** simply lets them **drop** to the ground

In Australia, one species of stick insect, called the spiny leaf insect, feeds almost exclusively on small, fleshy casuarina seeds, which are rich in oil and nutrients. Harvester ants like the seeds too and collect them. They store them in their nests and leave them to sprout. The female spiny leaf insect takes advantage of this by producing eggs that are small, round, and finely ridged, exactly like casuarina seeds. The harvester ants can't tell the difference, so they collect the insect's eggs along with the seeds and store them all together. Later, when the ants come to eat their stores, they find that only some of the seeds have sprouted tasty attachments. They eat only those and leave the eggs alone.

Eventually, the eggs hatch, and we might imagine that this would put the infant stick insects in considerable danger. They are, after all, uninvited intruders in the ants' nest. However, the stick insects' gift for mimicry protects the infants once again. When they hatch, they look and move exactly like newborn ants and simply walk out of the nest and climb up the casuarina tree to start the process again.

3
Crafty Critters

Which Creature
Can Drop Its Tail Off ?

Many types of lizard, including skinks, have the
ability to drop off their tails when threatened by a
predator. The tails have special fracture points, so
that if these lizards are being chased or grabbed
by a predator, the tail will drop off. Amazingly,
the tail will continue to wriggle, confusing the
predator and creating the illusion of a continued
struggle. With luck, this buys the lizard enough
time to escape.

In the weeks after losing a tail, the lizard will
usually be able to grow another, although this one
will contain cartilage rather than bone and will often be smaller than the original tail. Sometimes, if
the first tail doesn't drop off fully, the new tail will
grow alongside it, giving the lizard the freaky appearance of having two tails.

Glass lizards do something even more surprising.
Like skinks, they drop their tails when threatened.

But when a glass lizard's tail drops off, it breaks into a number of pieces—shattering like glass. A glass lizard's tail makes up as much as two-thirds of the creature's length, so it is a shocking and extraordinary sight when it shatters—it looks as if the creature has spontaneously smashed into pieces (and technically it has). Often the broken pieces of the

when a **glass lizard's** tail drops off, it **shatters** like **glass**

tail will continue to twitch while the glass lizard itself remains motionless, confusing and distracting the predator and helping the lizard make its escape.

Why Do Moles Squeeze Earthworms?

Moles are cute, furry, burrowing mammals that are around 6 inches (15 cm) long and weigh 3.5 ounces (100 g). They spend most of their lives foraging in a network of underground tunnels, through which they burrow at incredible speed.

Moles have short, powerful legs and very broad front feet, which they use for digging. Just one small mole can dig its way through an amazing 46 feet (14 m) of soil in only one hour.

Moles have an active, high-energy lifestyle, which means they usually need to eat their own weight in food each day. Their diet can include insects, spiders, grubs, and even an occasional mouse, but their main food is earthworms. When it finds an earthworm, a mole will pull it through its paws, squeezing it tightly to force out any earth and mud from the worm's guts.

Then the mole will either eat the worm or keep it for later. Moles have a toxin in their saliva that can paralyze earthworms, so they often bite off the worm's head, paralyzing but not killing it. They store the headless worm in a specially constructed underground room. Scientists have found well-stocked mole pantries containing as many as a thousand paralyzed earthworms.

How Do Fireflies Tell Fire-lies ?

Fireflies are celebrated for their wonderful ability to produce cold light (meaning that there is no heat emitted) through a process called bioluminescence, in which the light is produced by the reaction of two chemicals in the presence of oxygen. Female fireflies use these green, yellow, and pale red lights to attract a mate. They flash their lights in a distinct pattern that is unique to their species and acts as a signal to nearby males. This system helps the males and females of each species to find eligible partners and to avoid wasting time paying visits to fireflies of other species.

However, some crafty female fireflies have found a way around this system. *Photuris* fireflies, which are also known as "femme fatale fireflies," can copy the flash patterns of other species in order to attract these males. When the male flies down, he is

female fireflies use light to attract a mate

expecting to find a friendly and receptive female of his own species. Instead, he finds a hungry femme fatale, which quickly kills him and eats him for dinner.

Which Spider Looks Like a Blob of Bird Poop

There is a spider, appropriately known as the bird-dropping spider, that looks just like a lump of bird poop. It has a gray-and-white body, and it is usually found with its legs tucked in, curled up in a ball, sitting on a leaf, just where a blob of bird muck might land. It may not be pretty, but this disguise is far from unique—a number of caterpillars use a similar camouflage.

Why would any creature choose to look like bird poop? Well, first, it protects them from predators. This spider's most likely attackers are birds, which naturally avoid eating the poop of other birds. Second,

Why would any creature choose to look like bird poop?

it helps them hunt food of their own. The spider's prey are unlikely to see any threat in the common sight of bird droppings and so may come far closer than is good for them.

Which Spider Hunts Like a Gaucho ?

Gauchos are South American cowboys, who traditionally use a special technique for bringing down cattle. They use a throwing weapon called a *bolas,* which consists of a piece of rope with wooden or metal balls at each end and another ball tied to the middle. Gauchos can throw bolas with great skill at the legs of fleeing cattle, making them trip and fall.

In many parts of the world, including South America, the bolas spider uses a similar technique to snare its prey. It is about the size of a pea and colored black and white. When darkness starts to fall, the spider goes hunting. First it lays a line of nonsticky silk on the underside of a twig or leaf. Then it hangs from this line, using two of its legs.

Next it spins a line of sticky silk, about 1 inch (2.5 cm) long, with a sticky blob of silk at the end, like the weighted end of the bolas. Now the spider simply hangs there, dangling its line, which glints in the twilight.

In these first few hours of the night, the spider is hunting for cutworm moths. Eventually, one will appear. The moth may be attracted by the light glinting off the sticky silk. It is also attracted by the scent that the spider emits, which matches the perfume used in cutworm moth courtship. As the moth gets closer, the spider swishes the bolas, swiping the moth into its mouth. If the spider hasn't caught anything in about 15 minutes, it will reel in its line and eat it (perhaps because the line will have lost its stickiness).

Later, when these moths are no longer active, the spider rests until about midnight. Then it goes hunting again, but this time it has a new target: a moth called the smoky tetanolita. The spider now begins to produce a different scent, this one designed to attract its new prey, like a skillful fisherman varying his bait to catch a different type of fish.

Which Spider Builds a Life-Size Model of Itself **?**

Many types of spiders decorate their webs, and these decorations seem to serve a number of functions. Some spiders use silk ornaments to strengthen the web. Other decorations seem designed to make the web more visible, either to deter large animals from accidentally walking into it and destroying it or to attract prey. Scientists in Taiwan have recently observed one type of spider building a life-size replica of itself as a decoy to fool predators. No other creature is known to build a model of itself in this way.

A number of species of orb spider are known to decorate their webs with curious materials, including discarded egg sacs, plants, and the remains of prey. Until recently, this kind of decoration was believed to be used as camouflage. But scientists observing the spiders found that wasps were actually more likely to attack decorated webs than plain ones, suggesting that the decorations weren't very successful camouflage.

Observing another species of orb spider, *Cyclosa mulmeinensis*, on Orchid Island, off the southeast coast of Taiwan, the scientists noticed that it built pellets using egg sacs and dead insect bodies that were exactly the same size and shape as its own body. These pellets would appear to wasps to be the same color as the spider and to reflect light in the same way. When wasps attacked the web, more often than not they would attack the decoy rather than the spider, suggesting that while these decoys might attract more wasps than an undecorated web, they nonetheless made the spider safer overall.

Do Fish Fish for Fish

There's a type of fish that has a very crafty technique for catching its prey. It is called an

the bait is its own **tongue,** which is long and thin and wriggles like a **worm**

anglerfish because it uses bait just like a fisherman. However, the bait it uses is its own tongue, which is long and thin and wriggles like a worm. The anglerfish sits on a reef with its mouth wide open and its tongue wriggling, looking just like a juicy, tasty worm. When a curious fish comes closer, thinking it found a snack, the anglerfish sucks it into its mouth and enjoys a snack itself.

The anglerfish is the only fish that is known to use this technique, but there is a kind of turtle that does something very similar. The alligator snapping turtle is a big, ferocious predator that can weigh as much as 220 pounds (100 kg). Its jaws are hooked and have a sharp cutting edge made of horn. It is so fierce that if you approach it on land, it may well attack you.

The alligator snapping turtle lies at the bottom of a lake with its mouth open, using its tongue to tempt passing fish. Like the anglerfish, the snapping turtle has a long, thin, bright red tongue, which wriggles in such a way as to perfectly mimic a worm. The turtle's technique is slightly different from that of the anglerfish. Instead of sucking its prey into its mouth, it snaps its powerful jaws shut, often chopping the fish in half.

How Do Japanese Crows Crack Open Walnuts?

Carrion crows are found throughout the forests of Japan, as are walnut trees. Until recently, carrion crows had never been able to crack open those tasty and nutritious treats because their beaks were not strong enough. Many birds do manage to crack open similarly difficult foods by dropping them from the air—for example, bearded vultures live mainly on a diet of bone marrow, which they get by dropping bones from a great height, cracking them open. The similarly ingenious Egyptian vulture likes to eat ostrich eggs, which are full of nutrients, but their shells are very thick and difficult to crack open. So the vultures drop rocks onto the eggs, breaking the shells. Walnuts can be cracked open by being dropped, but they have to be dropped as many as 50 times, so it's a lot of work for a small snack.

In 1990, the ingenious carrion crows of Sendai City came up with an impressive solution. They started using cars. The birds wait at the city's traffic lights, holding walnuts in their beaks. When the lights turn red, they swoop down and place the nut in front of a car's tires. When the lights turn green, the cars drive over the nuts, cracking them open. The birds wait for the lights to turn red again, then hop back down into the road and pick up their dinner. This behavior is slowly spreading as other crows observe it happening and then take it up themselves. One of the most fascinating aspects of this behavior is that the crows seem to have learned to use traffic lights and to understand something of how they work, because other stretches of road would be too dangerous.

Why Do Birds Pretend to Be Injured?

Rather than build elaborate nests in trees, a number of birds, such as lapwings and plovers, simply lay their eggs on open ground—on marshes, grasslands, or beaches. This is a simpler solution than building an intricate nest, but it means the eggs are more vulnerable to predators such as foxes. One way to protect the eggs is to camouflage them, and so birds that nest in this way tend to produce eggs with mottled patterns to make them invisible against the gravelly ground. When the chicks hatch, the parent birds carry away the broken bits of shell so that their shiny white interiors don't attract predators.

This camouflage doesn't always work. If a predator gets close to the chicks, it's likely to recognize them as a meal, so the mother will try a different trick: she will pretend to be injured. When predators approach, lapwings and plovers hop away from their nests, dragging a wing along the ground as if they are hurt. To ensure that they attract the predator's attention, they may start screaming as if in pain or distress.

A predator such as a stoat is likely to be far more tempted by the prospect of a fully grown adult bird than a handful of eggs or chicks, and so it follows, getting gradually dragged away from the young birds. As the predator gets closer to the mother, at the last minute she suddenly flies away, as if she has been miraculously healed. However, the stoat has by now been led so far away from the nest that, even if it had spotted the eggs in the first place, it now has no way of retracing its steps and finding the eggs again.

Other birds seem to have developed this trick to an even more advanced degree. Instead of faking an injury, purple sandpipers on an Arctic tundra run away from their nests with both wings trailing behind, raising their feathers while making a squeaking sound that bears no resemblance to their usual calls. Thus, they look and sound just like a scuttling mouse or lemming, both of which are particularly tempting prey for arctic foxes, the most likely audience for the performance. In the United States, the green-tailed towhee also tries to mimic another kind of appealing prey. If a coyote approaches, it will run from its nest while lifting its tail. This at first glance makes it look a bit like a chipmunk, which is the main prey of local coyotes.

Do Animals Tell Lies ?

A number of bird species are known to deceive one another for their own gain, taking advantage of the communal warning system by which many birds depend on one another for their safety.

Often a forest will contain many species of birds of a similar size, which are all threatened by the arrival of a larger predator such as a hawk. Consequently, birds have developed a wonderfully resourceful warning system, in which the first bird to spot the danger will sound the alarm by giving a particular type of call, which is usually written as *seet*. It is a soft, short, high-pitched call, which is clear and easily understood but difficult to locate, thus minimizing the danger for the caller. (Obviously, an alarm call that significantly endangered the signaler would be of very limited value.) On hearing the *seet* call, all the birds in the area will drop what they are doing, find shelter, and remain quiet.

But this system also presents opportunities for deception. In the Amazonian rain forest, communities of small birds operate a warning system while they rummage through the leaf litter looking for tasty insects. Here two species of bird often keep watch: antshrikes, which perch under the shade of the canopy, and shrike tanagers, which act as lookouts above the canopy. Doing this job means that these birds have less time to forage for insects, so the other birds reward them by letting them have some of the insects that they find. Sometimes, though, the lookouts will lie. If they spot a particular tasty-looking insect being dug up, they may give a warning call even though there is no actual danger. The other birds will flee for safety, and the caller will come and grab the insect.

Various monkey species use a similar system

of alarm calls. Vervet monkeys have at least five different calls, which give detailed warnings as to which direction the danger is coming from, whether it is from the ground or the air, and how urgent and threatening the danger is. Again, however, sometimes the lookouts tell lies. In one example, researchers witnessed one monkey watching another monkey digging up a large root. Just as it was about to pull this tempting prize from the ground, the first monkey shouted the alarm for *snake,* which sent the other monkey scuttling up into the trees for safety. Then the crafty lookout came down and grabbed the tasty root, with no snake in sight. In a more detailed study, capuchin monkeys were found to do the same thing. In an Argentinean national park, scientists found that the monkeys sounded the alarm more frequently when pieces of banana were placed in the open.

Of course, the two main preoccupations of most creatures are food and reproduction, so as we might expect, there are also examples of animals that tell lies for the purposes of attracting a mate.

For instance, male domestic chickens are known to produce a specific type of call when they have found food. Sometimes these chickens give this call when in fact they have no food, purely to lure the female to come closer.

Which Bird Is an Expert Impressionist?

In the forests of southern Australia lives a bird with an extraordinary talent. It is the male Australian lyrebird, and it sings one of the most beautiful and complex songs of any bird. When it's time to mate, the female lyrebirds make a tour of the males' display mounds in the forest to inspect their potential partners. The males are extraordinary-looking, with cream-colored, fanlike tail feathers. When the males display, they bend these tail feathers forward, completely covering themselves.

At the same time, they sing a variety of songs, which are not only pleasing to the ear but also full of clever mimicry. The male lyrebird's courtship song incorporates many amazing trills and warbles and also mimics the songs of almost every other bird in the neighboring area. Ornithologists are said to be able to recognize the calls of more than a dozen different birds in the lyrebird's playlist. Presumably, this talent has evolved in response to the female's attraction to ever more complex and varied performances.

Perhaps the most impressive aspect of the lyrebird's act is that these songs are not just inherited traits, passed down through the generations. Rather, each individual bird has a talent for spontaneous mimicry and can quickly learn and incorporate new sounds. This is demonstrated by the great speed with which these birds add the sounds of human activity into their songs when their territories are close to human settlements. Lyrebirds observed near populated areas have been known to mimic the

lyrebirds mimic the sounds of **chain saws,** car alarms, **barking dogs,** camera motors, **car horns,** welding machines, and crying babies

sounds of chain saws, car alarms, barking dogs, camera motors, car horns, welding machines, and crying babies in their recitals. Some are also said to have learned tunes that they've overheard being played by musicians.

Why Do Owls Collect Poop

A large proportion of a burrowing owl's diet consist of dung beetles, and so these wise birds have come up with an ingenious way to attract their prey. Dung beetles, of course, love nothing more than poop; in fact, their whole society is based on it. Taking advantage of this, burrowing owls collect the droppings of cows, horses, and other large mammals and carry them back to their burrows, lining their nests with the smelly stuff. This bait attracts the dung beetles, which scuttle their way to the burrow's entrance, hoping for a tasty meal. Instead, they soon find that the hungry owl waiting there deserves its reputation for intelligence.

Which Bird Turns Itself into an Umbrella?

Green-backed herons are perhaps the craftiest fishermen of all the birds. They use a number of sophisticated techniques to catch their prey and are also able to quickly learn new tricks. One of the heron's clever techniques is to turn itself into an umbrella. On a hot day, a wading heron may spread its broad wings, creating a patch of cool, shady water in the lake or river where it is hunting. Remaining quite still, the heron then waits for a fish to swim into this pleasant patch of shade before grabbing it in its beak.

This is merely one of this particular heron's impressive fishing techniques. In Japan, green-backed herons seem to have recently learned to fish with bait, having presumably picked up the habit from observing humans. In a public park, where people come to feed the exotic fish, herons have started picking up morsels of bread and dropping them onto the surface of the lake, as if feeding the fish. When a hungry fish comes to the surface to take the bread, the heron grabs it in its beak. Herons have also been seen using insects as bait in the same way.

The heron also uses another even more sophisticated tactic. As fishermen will tell you, fish are naturally curious. It is not always necessary to offer food to get them to rise to the surface; something shiny or colorful will do the trick just as well. A bird called the little egret has black legs with bright yellow feet. To attract fish, the little egret shakes one of its brightly colored feet on the surface of the water, tempting fish to come to investigate. The green-backed heron has learned to do something similar, dangling small feathers on the water's surface, and this also seems to work.

Which Birds Can Chat with Badgers ?

The honeyguide is a small, dull-looking bird, distantly related to woodpeckers. It is found in Asia and Africa. The honeyguide likes to eat beeswax and bee larvae as well as other insects. In fact, it is the only animal of any kind that is known to be able to digest wax.

In Asia, bees tend to nest in relatively open, unprotected sites, hanging from the ceiling of a cave, for example. Honeyguides have no trouble raiding these nests.

But African bees tend to build their nests in tight places, such as holes in trees or small spaces between rocks. Honeyguides can find these nests, but they can't get in, so they recruit the help of a creature called a honey badger, also known as a ratel. Ratels love honey, and they have the necessary claws and physical strength to break into all kinds of nests. Amazingly, these two very different species have learned to work together.

When the honeyguide finds a ratel, it perches nearby and calls to it, giving a distinctive, chattering cry. The honey badger responds with a series of guttural growls and begins to follow the bird. The honeyguide flies off, frequently stopping, calling, and fluttering its tail at the ratel to make sure it's still following, while the ratel answers these calls by growling back. When the bird reaches the hive, it perches above the hive and gives a different call. The ratel apparently understands what this means—that the nest is nearby—and begins digging for it. Once the ratel finds the nest, the bees attack it, swarming around its head and stinging it. The ratel responds by farting into the nest hole, and the smell it produces must be as unbearable to the bees as it is to humans since most of the

the **ratel** responds by **farting** into the nest hole

bees now flee. Using its claws, the ratel tears out the honeycombs and carries them away. The honeyguide now swoops down to forage in what's left of the wreckage of the nest, feasting on the dead bees, grubs, and honeycomb.

Honey badgers are not the only animals that honeyguides have learned to work with. They also collaborate with humans, specifically the Boran people of East Africa. When they want to find honey, the Boran bushmen give a specific whistle, known as a *fuulido*, to summon the honeyguide. The bird will then lead them to a secluded bees' nest, just as it would lead a ratel. According to tradition, once the bushmen are finished, they leave a gift behind for the honeyguide to thank it for its help.

Which Animal Is Nature's Most Unlikely Impressionist

One candidate must be the tiny blister beetle larva, which manages to impersonate a creature hundreds of times its size. Or, rather, it manages to do so with the help of hundreds of its siblings. A bunch of blister beetle larvae group together into the beelike shape of a female digger bee to fool a male bee into trying to mate with them.

Why, you ask? To hitch a ride.

When the group attracts a male digger bee, rather than get crushed, the larvae climb onto the bee and cling to its body with their tiny claws. The bee, most likely confused, flies off to find another mate. When he finds one, the beetle larvae jump onto her. This is the last leg of their trip.

The fertilized female now returns to her nest, where she has filled a number of open cells with pollen. Here the beetle larvae dismount to enjoy their new home, where they will grow in safety, feasting on the bees' eggs and honey, before emerging as adult blister beetles.

Are Sheep Smarter Than We Think?

Sheep don't possess the most thrilling intellects of the animal kingdom, but they perhaps deserve more credit than they are given. For one thing, they have excellent memories. They can remember the faces of sheep and people for up to two years. They can also be trained to remember the rocks and streams that mark the boundaries of their territory and then pass on this information to their young. This is obviously an extremely useful trait from a shepherd's point of view. Some flocks of sheep will retain this information for centuries, passing it on from one generation to the next.

Sheep have also displayed some even more daring talents. Recently, for example, sheep in Yorkshire, England, have taught themselves how to roll across cattle grids to raid the local villagers' gardens. Daredevil sheep have been observed getting a running start and then rolling across the hoof-proof grids in a ball like army commandos. Since these grids are about 8 feet (2.5 m) wide, this is no mean feat. The hungry sheep are also said to have learned to climb or hurdle over fences up to 5 feet (1.5 m) high. So you see, not all sheep are sheepish!

daredevil sheep have been observed rolling across hoof-proof grids in a ball like army commandos

How Do Stoats Hypnotize Rabbits?

There is a type of weasel called the stoat that is one of the animal kingdom's most extraordinary predators. They eat a varied diet, including birds, eggs, insects, and small mammals. They also hunt rabbits, even though rabbits are much bigger than stoats and can weigh 10 times as much. Rabbits are also strong, alert, agile, and very fast, which makes them an extremely difficult meal to catch. However, stoats have learned how to get around all of these challenges—by using hypnosis.

The stoat stealthily approaches the rabbit, creeping toward it through the long grass. When it gets within range, it deliberately draws attention to itself, dancing, jumping, and chasing its tail. It's a bizarre performance. The stoat somersaults, then backflips. It vanishes into the grass, then leaps up in the air again. The rabbit is mesmerized as the dancing stoat gradually gets closer and closer. Suddenly, the stoat leaps toward the rabbit and bites into the back of its neck, smashing the back of its skull with its teeth. The rabbit may twitch once or twice before collapsing, dead. The businesslike stoat now drags the heavy corpse back to its burrow.

Which Bird Builds a Decoy Nest?

In the Australian bush, a type of bird called the yellow-rumped thornbill is terrorized by currawongs, which are big, aggressive birds that attack the thornbills' nests and steal their eggs. Their solution is to build a second, decoy nest on top of the active one. The decoy nest is simple a cup-shaped depression, while underneath it sits the real nest, with a hidden entrance. Currawongs attack from above, so if they see the empty decoy nest, they are likely to leave it alone and move on without investigating further, unaware of the active nest underneath. Thanks to this clever construction, thornbill nests suffer far less from currawong raids than their neighbors' do.

How Do Squirrels Deceive Rattlesnakes?

A squirrel's tail is one of the most useful tools of any mammal's. First, squirrels use their tails to balance when walking along a precarious branch. If they do fall, their tail acts as a parachute, catching the air and slowing the squirrel's descent. When running on the ground, squirrels use their tails as a fifth limb and rudder to help them change direction at speed. If a bird attacks, a squirrel can shelter under its big bushy tail, making it impossible for the bird to grab it in its talons. In the summer, a tail makes an effective sunshade, while in the winter, it's like a wonderfully soft, warm quilt, which helps the squirrel to conserve precious heat and energy.

Another exciting use for the squirrel's tail has recently been discovered. Snakes are one of the squirrel's most dangerous predators, but squirrels have found a way to use their tails to protect themselves against one group, namely the rattlesnake. Rattlesnakes have a poor sense of sight, but they have another way of "seeing" their prey, using their extremely sensitive heat-sensing organs. These organs consist of two small pits, one on either side of the snake's head, between its eyes and its nostrils. These pits help snakes detect the size, shape, distance, and direction of prey purely from sensing its heat energy.

When a squirrel is confronted by a rattlesnake, it fills its tail with blood, raising the tail's temperature. Since the rattlesnake can only really see things if they are warm, this makes the squirrel look twice as big as it otherwise would, which can be enough to make the rattlesnake warily slink off, leaving the squirrel in peace. The most amazing part of this ingenious technique is that squirrels don't bother to heat up their tails for other snakes. They do it solely for snakes that have these heat-sensing organs.

What Is Particularly Devious About the Alcon Blue Butterfly

The Alcon blue butterfly (*Maculinea alcon*) is an extremely attractive specimen that is found in Europe and northern Asia, where it brightens up many summer afternoons. However, as delicate and charming as they look, Alcon blues are among nature's most devious schemers when it comes to raising their young.

The process begins when the butterfly lays its eggs on the leaves of a gentian plant. When the caterpillars hatch from the eggs, they burrow into the flower's buds and feed. They grow much larger and eventually drop to the ground. Here the caterpillar is found by ants. At this point, the caterpillar begins to produce a chemical pheromone, which somehow seems to induce the worker ants to treat it like one of their own precious larvae. The ants take the caterpillar back to their nest and begin to feed it.

Yet the caterpillar is not satisfied with food and safe lodgings. Now its chemical signals instruct the ants to give it preferential treatment. If the nest is disturbed, the ants will rush the caterpillar to safety while ignoring their own young. For an astonishing two years, the ants will continue to feed the interloper until it is fully grown and ready to take its adult form. When it emerges from its pupal stage, the butterfly is at last recognized for the imposter that it is.

This story of deception and intrigue has one more amazing twist. The butterfly does not always make it to its adult stage because another crafty creature may further complicate things. While the alcon blue is still a caterpillar, a female ichneumon wasp may appear. This parasitic wasp seems to be able to sense when an ants' nest is hosting an alcon blue. When the wasp enters the nest, the ants panic and try to attack her. In response, the wasp emits a powerful pheromone of her own, which not only repels the ants from her but also makes them attack one another. In the confusion, she lands on the caterpillar and injects an egg deep inside its body.

After the wasp flies off, the ants continue life as normal. They feed the caterpillar as attentively as always, and it eventually turns into a chrysalis. But when the chrysalis opens, it's not an alcon blue butterfly that emerges but an ichneumon wasp, which has devoured the butterfly pupa from the inside out!

4
Mind-Boggling Biology

What Happened to
the Exploding Toads of Hamburg ?

In April 2005, strange reports started to come out of Hamburg, Germany. According to local people, toads around a pond had begun to explode spontaneously, as many as a thousand in a matter of days. According to reports, the toads were seen crawling on the ground as their bodies gradually swelled to the bursting point. Then they would explode, propelling their entrails up to 3 feet (1 m) into the air. Local people began to worry, and the authorities warned that children and dogs should be kept away from the area. The pond itself was sealed off and became known as the "pond of death."

So what was causing this bizarre phenomenon? Were local people imagining it? Was it some kind of elaborate hoax? Or was there a more logical explanation? Scientists speculated that the cause could be some unknown virus or fungus in the pond; there had been cases of foreign horses at a nearby racetrack becoming infected by a type of fungus. Other suggested explanations included the over-use of pesticides and increased ultraviolet radiation caused by the thinning of the ozone layer.

One of Germany's top experts on amphibians, Franz Mutschmann, decided to investigate. He began collecting the toads' carcasses and performing autopsies on them. He noticed that all of the toads were missing their livers and that each had a precise circular incision on its back, small enough to be the work of a bird's beak. He concluded that crows were attacking the toads and tearing out their livers. In response, the toads would fill themselves with air as a defense mechanism. But instead of deflating like they usually do, the toads' blood vessels and lungs ruptured, sending their intestines flying into the air.

But why were the crows taking just the toads' livers rather than eating the whole creature? Crows know that toads' skin is poisonous, so they worked out how to get a snack without eating the skin.

Why Are Poison-Dart Frogs Endangered?

The amazing poison-dart frogs of Central and South America produce some of the most toxic poisons of any animals. The frogs are so toxic that they have few predators. They have developed extremely bright, vividly colored skins to attract mates and to alert any potential predator to the danger they pose.

The most lethal of them all is perhaps the golden poison frog, which is believed to be the world's most poisonous vertebrate. The frog is just 2 inches (5 cm) long, but it contains enough poison to kill between 10 and 20 adult humans. The tiniest drop of this poison will disable a person's nervous system, causing the muscles to contract uncontrollably, leading to heart failure. Chickens and dogs have been killed simply by coming into contact with a paper towel that one of these frogs had walked across.

One might imagine that a creature with such emphatic defensive attributes would face few

to survive all the other dangers facing an aging large mammal will nonetheless die of starvation.

Do Any Animals Take Medicine?

A number of mammals have learned how to be their own doctors. Chimpanzees eat the bristly leaves of the *Aspilia* plant, which contains a special oil that kills the bacteria, intestinal worms, and other parasites that can infect their stomachs. The chimps pluck off the plant's leaves, mash them up in their hands, and chew them before swallowing. The leaves have little or no nutritional value, so the only reason to eat them seems to be their medicinal value. This theory is supported by the fact that the chimps seem to find the taste bitter, because when they eat the leaves, they pull faces and give other indications of an unpleasant taste.

In another example, Rwandan mountain gorillas travel to special parts of the forest where they eat fistfuls of the earth, which is rich in special minerals that their normal diet lacks.

dangers, and yet many species of poison-dart frog are actually endangered. Ironically, the frogs' very toxicity may be the reason. The indigenous people of the Amazon rain forest have learned to harvest the frogs' poison by catching them, roasting them on a spit, and collecting the poison as it drips from their skin. The resulting sticky paste is then used to tip their arrows for hunting trips or warfare.

Which Beetle Seeks Out Fire?

What would you do if a raging forest fire was heading straight toward you? You'd probably want to get away as quickly as possible. However, one bizarre little beetle does the opposite. The black jewel beetle, also known as the firebug, can sense the faintest whiff of a forest fire at great distances. And when it gets the scent, it heads straight for the inferno.

when the **black jewel beetle** gets the scent of a fire, it heads straight for **the inferno**

The reason is that the black jewel beetle likes to make its home in the charred trees, ideally as soon as possible after a fire. Most creatures either flee a fire or die, which means that a charred tree is likely to be free of any predators. This means that a hot, charred tree provides a haven where the black jewel beetle can mate recklessly and lay its eggs safely without fear of predators or competition.

The way the jewel beetle senses a distant fire is fascinating and not yet fully understood. The beetle has a tiny infrared sensor under one of its legs, which allows it to detect the faintest whiff of wood smoke from as far as 50 miles (80 km) away. Scientists are hoping to harness this amazing technology to develop an early-warning system for forest fires.

Why Do Elephants Die of Hunger?

Elephants graze on the open plains of Africa and Asia, eating a fibrous diet of grass and leaves. This wears down their teeth very quickly. Othe[r ani]mals with a similar diet face the same pro[blem] which they deal with in a variety of ways. Rab[bits] for example, have teeth with open roots that c[on]tinue growing throughout their lives to replace [the] constant wear at the other end.

Elephants' teeth grow in a different way. Mo[st] mammals' teeth emerge vertically from the jaw but elephants' teeth come in from back to front. As the old teeth are worn away, the elephants' new molars emerge at the back of the jaw and gradually push through to the front until the old ones drop out. There is a limit to how many sets of teeth an elephant can produce. After its last pair is worn out, the animal is unable to produce any more teeth, and even if it is healthy and capable in all other respects, with no way of chewing its food, it starves to death.

Elephants are not alone in this: kangaroos too have a limited number of sets of teeth. Kangaroos can produce only four pairs of molars. Once these are worn away, any kangaroo that has managed

In the Amazon rain forest, macaws peck at exposed banks of mineral clays to get essential minerals. Sheep too have been shown to seek out certain foods to make them feel better. When given a diet high in acids, which can cause digestive problems, sheep will actively choose foods that contain substances that help to soothe their system. Furthermore, tests have shown that sheep with specific digestive problems will be more likely to select just the right foods to make them feel better.

an overturned shark goes into a **comalike** state for 15 minutes

What Happens If You Turn a Shark Upside Down?

If you turn a shark onto its back, it will become completely immobile. For some reason, an overturned shark goes into a comalike state (called tonic immobility) for 15 minutes, during which it remains totally unresponsive. Its dorsal fins straighten, and its breathing and muscle contractions become more steady and re-laxed. No one knows the reason for this strange re-action, but even the scent of food is not enough to wake the shark once it is in this state.

Why Do Rhinos Charge into Trees ?

Rhinos have very poor eyesight, which makes it difficult for them to spot danger. Consequently, they have developed what to us might seem to be a rather silly response. When they spot anything that looks remotely like danger, they will charge at it, even if it means they end up crashing into trees or boulders. Despite their bulky size, rhinos are amazingly quick, charging at speeds of up to 28 miles (45 km) per hour, which is faster than even the top speed of the world-record-breaking Jamaican sprinter Usain Bolt.

rhinos charge at speeds of up to 28 miles per hour, faster than **Usain Bolt**

Why Do Ostriches Eat Stones ?

Anyone witnessing an ostrich picking up and swallowing mouthfuls of grit and stones might think it isn't too smart. But this collection of gravel actually serves a crucial purpose.

One of the defining features of birds is that they have a beak rather than a mouth full of teeth. Beaks are light, powerful, and aerodynamic, but they are no good for chewing, and a bird's food is often swallowed whole. Luckily, deep inside its stomach, birds have a second chamber called the gizzard. A gizzard looks like a flat, round purse, with thick, ridged walls that contract rhythmically to grind the bird's food and break it down (with the help of digestive juices produced by the stomach's first chamber).

In fact, all birds have a gizzard, but birds that live on seeds need extra abrasive power to break down the seeds, so they fill their gizzard with grit. Grit weighs less than a mouthful of teeth, and its location in the stomach is more aerodynamic and better balanced for flight. Nonetheless, the extra weight is still a consideration, so some birds get rid of their grit at certain times of the year when their diet switches to insects. Birds that spend very little time in the air, such as turkeys, chickens, and ostriches, have large gizzards that contain a lot of grit.

5
Vicious Varmints

What's the Best Way to Fight a Crocodile?

Crocodiles are one of the most enduring species on earth, and for good reason: they are ferocious predators. If you're faced with a crocodile, your best bet is to get away as quickly as possible. The fastest crocodiles can run at only about 11 miles (18 km) per hour, which is slower than most people can sprint, so on land a person should be able to run away from a crocodile. It could also help to run from side to side since crocodiles are not good at making sharp turns. But don't climb a tree to escape. Crocodiles are incredibly patient and will wait under a tree for days if they are likely to get a good meal out of it.

However, crocodiles live and hunt in the water, so that's where an attack is most likely to take place. If that happens, it's said that the best thing to do is attack its eyeballs with your fingers. Apparently, the crocodile will

> **crocodiles will wait under a tree for days if they are likely to get a good meal out of it**

automatically open its jaws and let you go since the eyes are the most sensitive part of its body.

A 26-year-old man named Hillary Amuma tested this theory when he was attacked by a crocodile while fishing in the Tana River in Ethiopia. The crocodile grabbed his left thigh and began to drag him into the water. Amuma says at that point he remembered the traditional Pokomo tribe method his grandfather had taught him. He threw away his fishing gear and jabbed his fingers into the crocodile's eyes. The animal let Amuma go but then got him again. Once more Amuma attacked the crocodile's eyes, and this time he escaped. "The Pokomo say a crocodile fears being touched in the eyes, and once that is done, it becomes immobile and lets go," he said. "A real Pokomo man cannot be scared by a crocodile."

Which Spider Crushes Its Prey to Death?

Many spiders have elaborate and clever ways of catching their prey. Some build sticky webs for insects to walk into or throw small webs over their prey. Others jump onto their prey, or chase it, or ambush it. One species builds a trapdoor and suddenly appears as if from out of the earth. Another spider mimics ants so that it can then eat them. One even hunts underwater. But once these predators have caught their prey, they all tend to kill it in the same direct fashion: they bite it, paralyzing it with their venom, and then devour it with their sharp, powerful fangs.

Hackled orb weaver spiders have no fangs, which means they have no way of paralyzing their prey. Instead, to kill a single moth or beetle, this spider will weave more than 460 feet (140 m) of silk, performing more than 28,000 individual movements to wrap its prey tighter and tighter. This silk shroud becomes so tight that it breaks the insect's legs and forces its eyes into its head, often killing it outright. The hackled orb weaver is the only spider known to crush its prey to death in this way.

Which Fish Spits Its Prey to Death ?

The archerfish has a very impressive technique for catching its prey. It is unique among fish because it can squirt precise jets of water from its mouth to shoot insects down from the waterside leaves and stems where they perch. The archerfish can spit up to 10 feet (3 m). It is extremely accurate, almost always hitting its target with the first shot. This is particularly impressive when you consider that the archerfish is underwater, which means that its view of the insect is refracted and distorted by the water's surface. Somehow the fish takes this into account when it aims.

Then, within 100 milliseconds of the insect's being knocked off its perch, the fish will start swimming to the exact spot in the water where it knows the insect will fall. Amazingly, the archerfish can predict this so accurately that it arrives to collect the insect just 50 milliseconds after it hits the water, ensuring that no other predator can sneak in and steal the fish's meal.

Which Bird Kicks Its Prey to Death ?

The secretary bird has an unusual way of killing its prey—it stamps its victims to death. It is an extremely tall, gangly bird that can reach 4 feet (1.2 m) in height. It can fly if necessary, but it has largely lost the habit, probably because it is so successful at hunting on the ground. It stalks across the grassland of Africa, often walking as much as 15 miles (24 km) a day.

Its main food is snakes, which it kills by kicking them in the head with its talons, but it also eats a wide range of other ground dwellers, including rats and insects.

Which Wasp Makes a Spider Spin It a Cocoon ?

There is a Costa Rican wasp, called *Hymenoepimecis argyraphaga,* that has an amazing way of getting its cocoon built. The process starts when the female wasp approaches a *Plesiometa argyra* spider. This is an enormous, fearsome spider that most insects sensibly avoid, but not this one. Instead, the wasp hovers in front of the spider and then lands directly on it. Then it quickly brings its ovipositor forward and implants an egg on the spider's back before swiftly flying off.

The spider seems to be unharmed, but as the egg develops, it remains on the spider's body, absorbing nutrients from its host. The night before the wasp larva pupates, the spider will destroy her own web. So far this is fairly normal behavior: most web spinners regularly destroy their webs, eating the silk and thus recycling it.

a female wasp lays her egg on the spider's back

However, the wasp larva has injected the spider with a chemical that makes the spider spin a new web that will be very different from her usual orb web. This web has none of the usual features—

no radial spokes and no sticky spirals. Instead, it is attached to the surrounding plants by extra-strong, reinforced threads. Unknowingly, the spider is building the last web it will ever produce. Once it is completed, the spider sits motionless underneath it and never moves again. The chemical from the wasp larva now kills the spider.

The wasp larva now feasts on the spider's body, eventually dropping the dry, empty husk. At dawn, the wasp spins its own bright orange cocoon, which hangs inside the spider's final web, elevated and protected from ants and Costa Rica's heavy rainstorms.

Can Bugs Act Like Soldiers?

Siafu, which are also known as driver ants, Matabele ants, or safari ants, are one of the fiercest and most dangerous of all insects. They are found mainly in Africa, where they live in large colonies. They have enormous jaws and eat a varied diet that includes insects, earthworms, termites, and sometimes even larger animals, including weak or injured mammals.

They travel in raiding parties several hundred strong, marching in columns, about six abreast. Alongside the soldiers run minors, which are about half their size. Earlier, a scout will have laid down a scent trail to lead them to their target, such as a termites' nest. As they march, they "sing" by rubbing a patch of ridges on their front.

When they reach the termite hill, they will be faced by ranks of soldier termites. These are bigger than the siafu, with huge, armored heads and powerful jaws, but nonetheless they are no match for the siafu. The siafu seize the termites and quickly inject their venom into the termites' brains, killing them within seconds. The raiders now start to make a pile of the vanquished termites.

With no guards left, the termite nest is now defenseless. The siafu storm inside, killing all the soft-bodied worker termites they can find. For a quarter of an hour, the slaughter may continue as the pile of bodies grows. The minors now start to carry the bodies back to their nest, carrying as many as six at a time. Eventually, the army marches back home, this time singing a different song, presumably a triumphant song of victory.

Which Bird Attacks in Squadrons?

Fieldfares are one of the largest members of the thrush family and are found in Europe and northern Asia. They are fairly large birds, around 9 to 10.5 inches (23 to 27 cm) long, which feed on insects, berries, and earthworms. They are sociable birds that often nest together in colonies. Like many birds, they alert one another to the arrival of a predator.

Say a chick stealer such as a magpie comes along. The first fieldfare to spot the threat will give a call, sounding the alarm. Rather than simply rushing for cover, the rest of the birds will take up the cry themselves, so that it quickly becomes an unnerving cacophony. They then dive-bomb the predator, shrieking at it as they swoop down, releasing bombs of feces. Fieldfares are adept at aiming these bombs, and many of them will hit their target. The magpie may soon end up covered in feces, making it fall to the ground, where it will hop away, dejectedly, to clean itself.

Which Crustacean Has a Hidden Switchblade

The mantis shrimp lives in shallow tropical and subtropical seas. Its main claw has a sharp extension that it keeps folded out of sight, a bit like a closed switchblade. When hunting, the mantis shrimp flicks open this claw extension at enormous speed and smashes it into its prey. It is one of the fastest physical movements that any animal is known to produce. A large Californian mantis shrimp, which is about 10 inches (25 cm) long, can have a strike speed of 33 feet (10 m) per second, which is about the speed of a bullet fired from a rifle. This strike is powerful enough to cut small

> a large Californian mantis shrimp can **smash** its main **claw** into its prey at the **speed** of **a bullet**

fish in two or crack open the shells of crabs and shellfish. Mantis shrimps are therefore not recommended as pets because their amazing weapon has been known to crack the side of a double-walled safety-glass fish tank.

Which Crustacean Kidnaps Creatures for Protection?

The resourceful hermit crab uses entire creatures as weapons. A hermit crab will attach a sea anemone to the back of its shell. Sea anemones have vicious, stinging tentacles, which serve to keep any predators far away from the hermit crab.

The little boxer crab takes this innovation even further. It carries a small anemone in each of its two front pincers and brandishes them like swords. If any predator threatens the crab, it thrusts its pincers forward, wielding its two bunches of stinging tentacles. The crab never lets go of its anemones, which means it is unable to use its front pincers to pass food into its mouth as most crabs do. Instead, it has learned to use its two front legs for this purpose.

Which Worm Captures Its Prey by Covering It with Glue ?

The answer is the velvet worm, which, in fact, is not even a worm. It looks a bit like a caterpillar, with a long, segmented body and between 13 and 43 pairs of stumpy feet. Velvet worms are usually around 2 inches (5 cm) long and are found in most tropical climates. However, they are very wary creatures and avoid light, so they are rarely seen. They have a fascinating evolutionary history. They are believed to have existed largely unchanged for 500 million years and may represent an evolutionary link between arthropods—that's the group that includes insects and spiders—and annelids, such as earthworms.

Velvet worms tend to live in dark, damp, secluded places such as caves, rotting logs, and leaf litter. They are cute, colorful creatures, but they are also voracious predators. They hunt at night, often killing prey much larger than themselves, including crickets, termites, wood lice, and spiders. The worms capture their prey by covering it in a sticky glue, which they shoot from two powerful tubes next to their mouth. Velvet worms can fire this glue up to 1 foot (about 30 cm). As the glue flies, it dries in the air before entangling the unfortunate victim, leaving it unable to escape. Now the worm will bite into its prey, injecting it with saliva that softens and liquefies the meal so it's ready to be devoured. The velvet worm will also eat the glue, which is rich in protein.

velvet worms can fire glue up to one foot

6
Weird Wonders

Why Do Penguins Look So Funny?

Penguins are naturally comic creatures that manage to be simultaneously cute and absurd-looking. But what is the reason for their unmistakable black-and-white feathers?

Well, it may look a little daft on land, but a penguin's coat is extremely practical. First, it protects the bird from its predators—sharks, killer whales, and seals, each of which can pose a threat only in the water. A penguin's coat helps to camouflage it while it swims. From above, its black back is hard to make out against the darkness of the ocean. From below, its white front is hard to pick out against the white of the sky.

The penguin's distinctive coloring is also useful for managing the bird's temperature, which is of vital importance for a creature living in the frozen Antarctic. When a penguin is cold, it will turn its black back to the sun to soak up as much of the sun's warmth as possible. When the penguin gets too hot, as unlikely as this may sound, it can turn its white belly to the sun to reflect the heat.

Why Don't Woodpeckers Get Headaches

Woodpeckers hunt for insects that few other birds can reach, hidden beneath the bark of trees. They do this by pecking at the bark with great force: each blow hits the tree at around 25 miles (40 km) per hour, and they peck up to 20 times per second. These blows are so powerful that if the bird's beak were not locked together by a special clasp, the two mandibles would fly apart.

A single one of these powerful whacks could knock the woodpecker unconscious if its force were to reach the bird's brain, but luckily the woodpecker's head is cleverly designed to cushion the blow. Woodpeckers have muscles at the base of their beak that act as shock absorbers. Furthermore, woodpeckers' brains are very small and suspended in fluid. Consequently, none of the impact reaches the brain, and so the woodpecker remains conscious.

Woodpeckers also have clever ways to protect themselves from flying splinters. Their nostrils are tiny slits that are protected by special feathers. And to stop splinters from getting in their eyes, woodpeckers close special membranes over their eyes a millisecond before each peck hits the wood.

Which Bird Can See Even with Its Eyes Closed

The potoo is an enormous bird that can reach more than 19 inches (0.5 m) in height and is found in the American tropics. Despite its size, even in broad daylight a potoo is almost impossible to see because it has amazing camouflage. The bird usually perches on top of a tree stump. It has brown, mottled feathers, which blend in perfectly with the tree's bark. If a predator approaches, the potoo takes further steps to make itself invisible.

It lowers its tail, pressing it flat against the bark of the stump so that there is no visible joint. It then lifts its head so that its beak is pointing vertically, making it look just like the broken end of branch, and closes its eyes.

Closing its eyes suggests that the potoo has considerable confidence in its camouflage. It will even stay completely still when a predator gets within 3 feet (1 m) of it. However, although

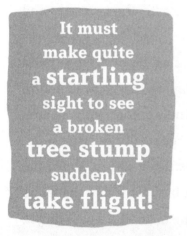

It must make quite a **startling** sight to see a broken **tree stump** suddenly **take flight!**

its eyelids are shut, the bird can still see faintly because its eyelids have two tiny vertical slits. They let through just enough light for the potoo to keep an eye on any approaching threat. If a predator does get too close for the potoo's comfort, it will suddenly take off and fly away. It must make quite a startling sight to see a broken tree stump suddenly take flight!

Which Butterfly Is an Escape Artist?

The hairstreak butterfly has a false head on its hind wings. The false head distracts birds from the butterfly's actual head and confuses them when the butterfly escapes, seemingly flying backward.

In fact, there are a number of other creatures that have false heads to confuse and deter predators. The shingle-back lizard, for example, has a large, stumpy tail that is exactly the same size and shape as its head.

There is also an amazing type of frog found in Chile, Brazil, and Uruguay that uses its entire body as a false head. The appropriately named four-eyed frog has two large swellings on its sides, which look just like eyes. They sit just above the frog's legs, and the overall effect is that the frog's whole body looks like the head of a much larger, more threatening creature. In addition, these false eyes are actually poison glands, so even if a predator does decide to bite the frog, the unpleasant taste will usually make it let go pretty quickly.

How Does a Snake Swallow an Antelope ?

Snakes are some of the most astonishing predators on earth. There are more than 2,900 species of snake, and all of them are carnivorous hunters despite their apparent lack of advantages. Snakes have no legs to chase their prey with, no hands to grab with, and no teeth with which to chew. Most species of snake can't even see particularly well. And yet they are found on every continent except Antarctica, and they prey on animals many times their size, including cats, pigs, and even antelope. How do they do it?

Most snakes kill their prey in one of three ways. Some use constriction—wrapping their body around the prey, tightening their grip every time the victim exhales until eventually it is unable to breathe in. Some snakes kill using their venom. More often, though, snakes use their venom to paralyze and subdue their prey before swallowing it whole.

Snakes are able to swallow creatures more than three times larger than their own heads, which is somewhat equivalent to our being able to swallow a basketball whole. A snake is able to do this because its skin and body are extremely elastic, and its skeleton doesn't limit the size of food that can be passed down its body. Snakes can also open their jaws to as much as 130 degrees, whereas the human jaw can reach a maximum angle of only 30 degrees. Also, a snake's lower jaw has two halves, left and right, which are connected by a flexible, elastic ligament, allowing them to be stretched apart.

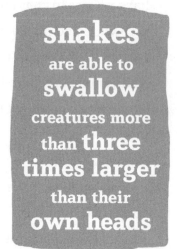

snakes are able to swallow creatures more than three times larger than their own heads

Snakes have no teeth to chew with, so they have to swallow their food whole. They swallow their prey headfirst because creatures such as birds, hedgehogs, and goats have feathers, spines, and horns, which could provide resistance or cause injury if ingested the wrong way around. Snakes have strong cheek and throat muscles with which they push their prey down to the stomach in a process that can take several hours.

Once the food reaches the stomach, the process of digestion can begin. If the meal is a big one, digestion can take a long time. Sudden movements may be risky if the meal includes spiky things such as spines, claws, or horns, so the snake will now try to lie low, out of the way, moving as little as possible.

A large meal will cause the snake's body to undergo substantial changes to facilitate the process of digestion and storage. Its heart will swell by 40 percent, and its liver may double in size. It can take more than a week for a snake to digest a large meal. Then, when digestion is finally completed, the snake's internal systems enter a dormant state, with significantly reduced functions, to conserve energy.

In this way, snakes can swallow creatures many

times their size. An African rock python was once observed swallowing a 130-pound (59-kg) antelope. There are also reports of snakes swallowing alligators whole and even human beings. In one recent example, in Indonesia, an entire human body, covered in slime and digestive juices, was said to have been cut out of a python.

Which Frog Has a Visible, Beating Heart

A tiny frog called the glass frog is found in many parts of Central and South Americas. Glass frogs range from around 1 to 3 inches (3 to 8 cm) in length and look a bit like tree frogs, with attractive lime-green skin on their backs. But if you turn the frog over, you will see something quite astonishing. The skin of the glass frog's front is transparent, allowing you to see its internal organs at work: its liver, digestive tract, even its beating heart and circulating blood.

Which Tadpole
Changes Shape to Foil Its Predator ?

There is a species of frog called *Rana pirica* whose tadpoles have evolved a unique way of protecting themselves from predators. The tadpoles can sense whether or not their predators, which are salamander larvae, are nearby. If the tadpoles sense the presence of a predator, they transform themselves into a different, bulging body shape, which makes them too big for the salamander larvae to fit into their mouths. Then if the predators leave, the tadpoles will return to their normal size.

However, the salamander larvae have developed an equally impressive response. If they sense the presence of the *Rana pirica* tadpoles, the salamander larvae will also change their shape, with their heads becoming much broader, allowing them to swallow the enlarged tadpoles.

Which Insect Grows a Fake Ant on Its Back ?

Dangerous creatures tend to have distinctive markings because it is important that they be recognized as dangerous. Honeybees, for example, carry a sting that can be deadly for many of their potential predators. However, if it is forced to actually use its sting, the bee itself will die. Therefore, the bee has a distinctive black-and-yellow pattern, colors that are understood in nature to indicate poison, to scare predators away. Similarly, the poison-dart frogs of the Amazon have bright, colorful skins, which indicate that they are among the most poisonous creatures on the planet.

However, if this strategy works, then it opens up the possibility of mimicry. If looking like a bee is enough to keep predators away, then why should a creature actually bother to develop a poisonous sting, which costs considerable resources and energy? Thus, while bees, wasps, and hornets are actually dangerous, there are also numerous other insects that look just like them, but in fact carry no sting at all. For them, just looking dangerous is enough.

for some, just looking dangerous is enough

This mimicry is developed to an extreme degree by a small treehopper called *Heteronotus*, which is found in the forests of Central America. This bug has evolved with a full-scale model of an ant on its back. If you look at it from above, as a bird would do, all you will see is the black shape of an ant, with gaping jaws, a thin waist, and a black abdomen. Beneath this imitation is the treehopper itself, which has a normal treehopper abdomen and wings and looks in all other respects just like an average member of its family. Looking like an ant protects the treehopper from birds, for birds generally avoid eating ants because they taste awful, they have a hard exoskeleton, and they often sting or bite.

Why Do Zebras Have Stripes?

The reason why zebras have their distinctive stripes is one of nature's most enduring mysteries. Even today we are still not exactly sure, although a number of theories have been proposed. One long-standing theory holds that this pattern works as camouflage, breaking up the outline of the zebra on the open savannas of Africa, where it roams. Many scientists are far from convinced by this for the simple reason that zebras are quite eye-catching and do not seem to be well camouflaged at all. However, the zebra's main predator, the lion, is color-blind. So it is possible that the zebra's vertical stripes do camouflage it in tall grass, even though to our eyes its coloration may make it appear obvious.

Another theory suggests that the zebra's alternating bands of black and white stripes reflect heat in different ways, creating cooling currents of air over the zebra's body. Yet another theory proposes that the stripes confuse the visual system of the bloodsucking tsetse fly. At least one function does seem to have been convincingly demonstrated. Zebras' stripes vary significantly from one individual animal to another, and it's clear that the zebras do identify and remember other members of the group by these distinctive markings.

zebras' stripes vary significantly from one individual animal to another, and zebras identify and remember other members of the group by these distinctive markings

7
Extra-Disgusting Details

Which Frog Coughs Up Its Entire Stomach?

When they need to vomit, some frogs have an incredible technique. Instead of simply expelling the stomach's contents, as we do, they cough up their entire stomach. Then they carefully rinse it out with their right hand, push it back inside, and swallow it. Why do they always rinse it with their right hand rather than their left? Apparently, it is because the tissues that hold the stomach in place are shorter on the right side, which means that when the frog expels its stomach, it always hangs to the right, where it can be washed only by the right hand.

Do Snakes Fart?

Snakes scare off potential predators in a number of ways. They hiss at them, raise themselves up, puff up their bodies, or rattle their tails. Two types of North American snakes have another way of scaring off their enemies. The Sonoran coral snake and the western hooknose snake are both quite small, which makes it harder for them to be physically imposing. Instead, they fart, although the technical term is the rather more proper "cloacal popping." Each "pop" lasts for less than two-tenths of a second and may be repeated several times. Relative to their size, these snakes fart quite loudly: the farts can be heard up to around 6 feet (2 m) away and sound just like our own farts, although slightly higher-pitched.

the **technical term** for a **snake fart** is a **"cloacal pop"**

This may be why the farts are effective: they sound like the farts of animals large enough to scare off the snake's usual predators. In tests, the snakes were found to fart only when threatened. They do so using two sets of muscles to isolate a compressed bubble of air, and then release it to the outside in an explosive burst. Apparently, they sometimes put so much force into these farts that they fling themselves up off the ground!

Why Does the Australian Rainbow Pitta Decorate Its Nest with Wallaby Poo?

The rainbow pitta is an attractive and colorful Australian bird that is known as the "jewel of the forest." It is similar in size and shape to a thrush, reaching about 8 inches (20 cm) in length. It has a velvet black head and breast, with green upper parts and an electric-blue patch on its wing. The pitta is found in the steamy rain forests and tropical mangrove and eucalyptus forests of northern Australia, where it lives on a diet of snails, worms, and insects.

Rainbow pittas are shy, sensitive birds that are difficult to observe. They breed at the beginning of the rainy season, between October and March. They usually build their nests in trees but will also nest on clumps of bamboo, in thickets, on tree stumps, or even on the ground. Their nests are made of twigs and leaves, in the shape of a football. The interior of the nest is lined with fine leaves and is reached via an entrance hole in the side of the dome. Next to this entrance, the rainbow pitta will often lay a kind of doormat, which it makes out of wallaby poo.

As you can imagine, a doormat made of poop in a tropical climate can get a bit stinky, but the bird doesn't seem to mind. In fact, the stink seems to be the point. In the forests where the rainbow pitta is found, brown tree snakes are a significant threat. These snakes will eat the bird's eggs if they can find the nest, and they use their powerful sense of smell to search for them. Decorating their nests with pungent wallaby poo, which they collect from the forest floor, fools the rainbow pittas' slithering predators and protects their young.

> a **doormat** made of **poop** in a **tropical** climate can get a bit **stinky**

Which Bird Kills Its Enemies by Throwing Up on Them?

The fulmar is a large seabird that looks a lot like a seagull. The name *fulmar* means "foul gull," and the name is well deserved, because the fulmar's main mode of defense is to vomit disgusting yellow oil over its enemies. This vomit is not only unpleasant and smelly but also potentially lethal. Most of the fulmar's predators are birds of prey, including skuas, ospreys, and sea eagles. The fulmar's vomit sticks to their feathers, making them unable to fly. It can even cause them to drown.

In fulmar families, both parents go hunting at sea for up to 20 hours at a time, leaving their nests undefended. The chicks are obviously not strong enough to defend themselves against birds of prey in a conventional manner, but fulmar chicks are born with this amazing ability to vomit oil and to aim it with precision. At just four days old, they can puke as far as 18 inches (0.5 m), while older chicks can spew three times that distance. When they are born, the chicks even instinctively vomit at their parents until they learn to recognize them as family.

penguins' poop power is four times greater than a human being's

Why Are Penguins Such Powerful Pooers?

A group of European scientists recently conducted a study of penguin feces and found that the birds could expel their poop with a force of up to 60 kilopascals (a pascal is a unit of pressure)—four times greater than a human being's equivalent poop power. Furthermore, the penguins could expel their poop to a distance of 16 inches (41 cm).

It seems that the penguin has developed this unusual talent in order to avoid soiling its feathers or its nest. For this unusual research, the scientists in question were awarded an Ig Nobel Prize, which is a lighthearted science prize designed to honor scientific achievements that "make people laugh—then think."

Penguins are not the only power pooers out

there. Kingfishers and hornbills will back up to the entrance of their waterside tree hole to expel a stream directly into the river; the stream will usually be powerful enough to avoid leaving any streak or mark on the tree or the riverbank. This helps them avoid detection by predators. If their tree were marked with feces, their hole would be easily discovered.

One reason why birds are able to develop such a gift is that they produce their urine and feces in one single stream, making it runnier than the excrement of mammals. This technique not only protects the birds from detection by predators but also keeps their nests clean, limiting the risk of infection and disease.

Which Bird Disguises Itself as a Pile of Cow Dung ?

The nacunda nighthawk lives out on the open plains of Brazil. It is nocturnal and spends most of its days resting on the ground. There are no trees or bushes in which to hide from predators, so the bird seems to be completely exposed. But it has developed a cunning form of camouflage. When it crouches, it looks like a pile of unappetizing cow dung.

The curious thing about this is that cows are a fairly recent addition to the wildlife of Brazil. There were no cows in Brazil until just a few centuries ago, when they were introduced by European explorers. And there are no other large grazing mammals on the plains of Brazil that might produce something similar to cow poo. This raises a fascinating question: How did the nacunda nighthawk evolve to resemble a pile of cow poo if there were no cows around to produce poop for it to mimic? It could not have evolved this talent in just a few centuries.

Scientists do have a theory to explain this. Although there are no other large grazing mammals on the plains today, once upon a time there were. Around a thousand years ago, these grasslands were the home of giant sloths and great armadillos, which were the size of today's cows. These creatures have been extinct for centuries, but the fact of their existence raises the amazing possibility that the nacunda nighthawk's camouflage may actually be providing us with an accurate picture of what their dung looked like all those centuries ago.

Why Do Vultures Poop on Themselves?

Staying cool is a difficult art to master. The only animals with sweat glands are mammals, and not all mammals have them (cats, whales, and rodents, for example, have lost most or all of their sweat glands).

Birds lose heat by raising their down feathers to increase airflow to the skin. They also take baths and pant. Some birds, including vultures, also do something fairly disgusting to keep their temperature down: they urinate and defecate down their legs.

Birds have a single posterior opening called a cloaca, which means that their waste products all come out together. (This is why bird poop is often so runny, because it also contains the bird's urine.) It may sound gross, but this habit probably also helps keep the birds clean. Bird poop contains uric acid, which is an antiseptic. Having it on its own legs may therefore help keep a vulture free from germs after it has walked through a carcass.

Some cranes and storks approach the problem of temperature regulation in a slightly different way. Their chicks are reared on stick platforms in tropical climates, where the heat of the sun can be very damaging. To keep them cool, parents collect stomachfuls of water and vomit over their young, giving them a refreshing shower. Herons solve this problem in an even more unpleasant way—they simply poop over their young.

Which Insect Lives Off of Cows' Runny Noses?

This is the rather unpleasant diet of the face fly, or *Musca autumnalis*. Face flies are found throughout most of North America, Europe, and Asia and are a major pest for cattle and horses.

Face flies hibernate over the winter and then emerge in the spring. The females lay their eggs in fresh manure, and these eggs usually hatch within 24 hours. The maggots grow in stages while feeding on the manure and then move to nearby soil for the final stage of their development. Depending on the local temperature, an adult fly will emerge in about two to three weeks.

Adult face flies live and feed on cattle, dining mainly on the animal's facial secretions, including tears, nasal mucus, sweat, and saliva. They have abrasive, spongy mouthparts, which soak up these protein-rich secretions and also cause the animal's eyes to produce more tears, which in turn attract more face flies. They are not considered to be blood feeders because their mouthparts are not able to pierce the host's skin. But given the chance, they will feed on a wound opened up by other blood-feeding flies.

We humans suffer from a very similar pest. The

eye gnat is a type of tiny fly, less than a tenth of an inch (2 mm) in length, that is found in many hot climates, including the southern United States. In the summer, annoying eye gnats congregate around our eyes and noses to feed on the moisture.

Which Type of Ant Loves Hospitals ?

The pharaoh ant, which is commonly found in hospitals, is one of the smaller species of ant—workers measure just 0.08 inch (2 mm) long. These yellow-brown ants form large colonies in warm, indoor spots because they need a warm temperature in which to breed.

They particularly thrive in hospitals because they like to eat a diet rich in protein, and so they feast on bloody bandages, dressings, IV solution, and surgical wounds. They are trail-making ants that can communicate information about new sources of food and water to one another, which helps the population to spread. Because they seek out sources of water, they will often find their way to toilets, drains, and bedpans. This makes them a serious health risk because they can transmit diseases, infect food, and contaminate sterile materials.

What Happens at a Dung Beetle Wedding

Dung beetles love one thing above all others: poop. When a dung beetle finds a tempting pile of droppings, it sifts through it, looking for the best morsels. Having made its selections, the beetle will then start to roll its dung into a ball, which soon becomes considerably bigger than the beetle itself. It can roll a ball that is 50 times its own weight by climbing on top and manipulating it with its legs.

Skillful beetles can roll their dungball at speeds of up to about 46 feet (14 m) a minute. They need to travel quickly because dung is a precious commodity. Other dung beetles may well come along and try to steal it. To minimize the risk of being robbed, dung beetles will always travel in a straight line toward their burial hole. Amazingly, they navigate by using polarized light from the moon. With luck, the beetle will manage to bring its prize home to a safe burial spot, ready to provide a delicious source of food for many days.

Yet there is more to dung than just a delicious meal. Every aspect of dung beetle society revolves around poo. A male dung beetle will often woo a female by presenting her with a ball of dung. Together, the couple then roll the ball back to their new home, with him pushing and her pulling, in a bizarre kind of wedding ceremony. The

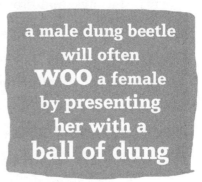

a male dung beetle will often **WOO** a female by presenting her with a **ball of dung**

female will then lay her eggs inside the dung ball, which provides an abundant source of food for their growth before the young eventually eat their way out.

Why Do Birds
Rub Ants into Their Feathers ?

Most animals that accidentally disturb a wood ants' nest soon come to regret it because the worker ants swarm out in an angry mob, squirting jets of acid at them from glands at the end of their abdomen. This is enough to repel most creatures, but some birds deliberately land on ants' nests and invite them to squirt.

Jays, starlings, and crows all enjoy sitting on ants' nests, in a process called "anting." As the angry ants swarm over them, the birds will fluff up their feathers, letting the ants discharge acid into every crevice. Some even pick up ants in their beaks and rub them over their feathers, as if squeezing out as much acid as they can get. The reason they do this is that the acid cleans the birds' feathers and rids them of any fleas, lice, or other skin parasites they might have picked up. Yet anting does not seem to be a purely functional chore. Many birds look like they enjoy it, cocking their heads back and closing their eyes, as if thrilled by the invigorating sting of the acid.

Birds are not the only creatures that enjoy the attentions of a raging ant swarm. Tortoises can't reach the top of their shells, making it impossible for them to remove any ticks or parasites that may have climbed on board. The North American wood tortoise uses ants to help keep it clean. It will simply walk into the ants' nest and sit still while the insects swarm all over it, squirting antimicrobial acid and killing any parasites they may come across.

Which Beetle Fires Really Smelly Stuff from Its Backside?

The pinacate beetle is a mean-looking black beetle that can reach up to around 1.5 inches (4 cm) in length. It is extremely hardy and is found in great numbers in the deserts of Mexico and the southwestern United States, where few other creatures can survive. Pinacate beetles even have a mountain range named after them, the Pinacate Mountains, on the border between Sonora (Mexico) and Arizona.

Pinacate beetles are also known as clown beetles because they do something bizarre when faced with danger. Rather than run away, these beetles will hurriedly stand on their head, often tumbling over into a somersault if they fail to balance properly. A beetle may flip over a number of times before settling into a controlled headstand. Although this display is entertaining, it's wise to take it as a warning. If the beetle continues to feel threatened, it may attack by shooting a disgusting, noxious chemical from its rear end, which it can fire up to about 30 inches (76 cm). For this reason, pinacate beetles have another nickname: they are also commonly known as stink beetles. This substance can cause painful burning and temporary blindness if it gets into your eyes, and it is extremely difficult to wash off.

However, a number of predators have figured out a

> when faced with **danger**, pinacate beetles will hurriedly stand on **their head**

way to take advantage of the stink beetle's abundance. Grasshopper mice teach their young to grab the beetle and stick its rear end into the ground, where it can't do any harm. Then they chew through the top half of the beetle. The beetle's other predators include burrowing owls, loggerhead shrikes, and, appropriately enough, skunks.

Why Do Hedgehogs Spit on Themselves?

Surprisingly, perhaps, given their prickly appearance, hedgehogs are regarded as one of the animal kingdom's cutest creatures. However, they have one very disgusting habit. A hedgehog will chew on the toxic skin of a toad, which produces poisonous foam, and then contort its body to spit the foaming saliva all over its own back. It's not clear why it does this, but presumably the foam is useful for deterring predators.

This habit may also help to explain how hedgehogs have developed such incredible immunity to poison. Hedgehogs can survive a bite from an adder, which would kill a guinea pig in five minutes. Also, it takes more chloroform to knock out a hedgehog than any other creature of similar size.

How Does the Brown Hyena Communicate Using Its Rear End **?**

In the Kalahari Desert, brown hyenas are constantly marking their territory, and they do this by a complex system of smelly deposits. They live in clans of about a dozen and travel long distances looking for food, which for the brown hyena consists of dead animal flesh and sometimes small mammals. Every few minutes, the hyena will "mark" by straddling a clump of grass and smearing it with oil from a gland near its rear end.

Other mammals mark their territory in a similar way, including civets, but the hyena's system has two parts. They produce a white paste that forms a small bead on the grass and an even smaller blob of black oil that sticks just above it. These two markers serve two very different functions. The white bead is a sign of ownership, warning hyenas of other clans that this territory is taken. This bead holds onto its powerful smell for several weeks. The black bead, on the other hand, is intended as a message for other members of the hyena's own clan. It loses its smell very quickly and vanishes within a few hours. If this bead's smell is strong, it lets any passing hyena know that this territory was patrolled recently and probably doesn't have any food left. If the scent is barely there or gone, the area might be ripe for hunting again. In any single clan's territory, there may be up to 15,000 of these whiffy signposts, and they are frequently updated.

How Do Rhinos Mark Their Territory ?

With poop, and lots of it! Some animals eat their dung; others bury it, hide it, or present it to their partner as a gift. But rhinos put it on display, in enormous piles more than 1 yard (about 1 m) across. Rhinos use these

rhinos put their poop on display

to mark the boundaries of their territory and may have as many as 30 piles dotted around, each of which they try to visit every day.

These piles serve two useful purposes. First, they notify rival rhinos that this territory is taken, warning them not to trespass. Second, they help the owner of the territory keep its bearings. Rhinos have very poor eyesight, so it's difficult for them to recognize landmarks. However, their sense of smell is excellent, so these dung piles serve as helpful olfactory markers.

Why Do Sloths Turn Green?

Sloths are medium-size mammals, usually about 20 inches (about 0.5 m) long, which live in the treetops in rain forests of Central and South Americas. The local tribes in Ecuador refer to sloths using three rather unkind names: *rittor*, *rit*, and *ridette*, which derive from the local words for "sleep," "eat," and "dirty." It's true that sloths do little more than eat and sleep, and they spend their lives hanging upside down from the branches of the trees in which they live. This is because their diet of leaves is very low in nutrients, so they have to expend as little energy as possible. Consequently, sloths have a much lower body temperature and metabolic rate than other mammals of a similar size.

The third accusation, that sloths are dirty, is sadly also true. A sloth's fur is a kind of yellowy-brown when the sloth is young, but as it gets older, its fur gradually turns green. This green color comes from a kind of algae that grows on the sloth's fur. Turning green is useful for the sloths. It helps camouflage them in the treetops, making it harder for predators to see them. The algae also contains lots of beneficial nutrients, so the sloth will frequently be seen snacking on lumps from its fur.

Which Bird Mugs Other Birds for Their Vomit?

The magnificent frigate bird is found around the coast of Australia and the Pacific islands. The *magnificent* in its name refers to is size—its wing-span is an enormous 6 feet, 6 inches (2 m)—but it could also describe the bird's aerial skills. The frigate bird is an amazing acrobat that can skim the surface of the sea to snatch fish using its hooked beak.

It also has another way of hunting that isn't exactly magnificent: it mugs other birds in flight to steal their vomit. The frigate bird can tell when another bird is flying home after a successful fishing mission. It will attack this bird in flight, perhaps tugging on its tail feathers. The victim, often a booby, will be knocked off balance and throw up its catch. The frigate bird then swoops into a dive and catches the regurgitated fish before it hits the water.

In Mexico, the aplomado falcon is another aerial pirate. Like the frigate bird, it is quite capable of catching its own prey, but studies have found that its odds of success are greater if it simply steals from other birds. Researchers found that the falcon's piracy attempts were successful 82 percent of the time, while actually trying to hunt for food itself produced positive results only 38 percent of the time.

Why Do Frogs Eat Their Own Skin

Frogs have soft, delicate skin that wears away quickly and has to be frequently replaced. Many frogs shed their skin as often as once a week. The process begins with a lot of twisting, bending, and stretching to loosen the old skin. The outer layer becomes separated from the new skin growing underneath and begins to split. The frog will scratch to loosen the outer layer with its forelegs, as if pulling off a scab (it may well itch and annoy the frog, just like a scab). At some point, the frog will be able to get part of the skin in its mouth, and then it will gradually pull the whole thing into its mouth, still loosening it with its legs, until the whole skin has been swallowed. Disgusting though this may sound, growing a new skin takes a lot of energy and nutrients, and so this way the frog gets to recycle the old skin. So you see, it's true: frogs really are green!

Which Creature Eats with Its Eyes

This is not a trick question. Frogs and toads put their eyes to work as they eat, and not only to watch out for threats or more food passing by. So how does it work? Well, they don't use their eyes as a mouth. They don't chew with them or ingest food through them. Instead, they use their eyes to push their food down into their stomach when they swallow. When a frog eats a tasty morsel, such as a small cricket, it will close its eyes and retract its eyeballs into its body. These push into the frog's pharynx, against the cricket, and repeated pushes gradually force the food down to the back of the frog's esophagus.

Why Do Dogs Eat Poop ?

Pet owners often report that their dogs will not stop eating poop, no matter how well they're fed and cared for. There's no clear consensus as to why they do this, although there are many theories. Some say the dog may be lacking certain nutrients. Others suggest that the dog may be under stress or seeking attention from its owner. Another theory is that the dog is trying to hide the scent of its poop to avoid attracting predators. Yet another theory holds that because most domestic dogs have been punished for pooping in the wrong place at some point, this may be their attempt to hide the evidence.

There may be no conclusive answer yet, but we do know that eating poop is not confined to dogs. A great number of animal species regularly eat their own poop, including rabbits, Japanese hares, northern pika, sportive lemurs, koalas, possums, chinchillas, European beavers, guinea pigs, and Norway lemmings.

Rabbits routinely eat their own leavings—for them it's simply one stage of the digestive process. A rabbit's diet consists of grass, leaves, and other plant matter. This is a diet that is low in nutrients and difficult to digest. To ensure that they are getting as much energy and nutrition out of their food as possible, rabbits eat their poop as soon as it emerges. This lets the rabbit's stomach give the food a second digestive processing. The round dry pellets that you see in a rabbit warren are what's left after the rabbit has digested its food twice.

Other animals are believed to eat their poop for a rather different reason. Many bird species are particularly careful about hiding their poop for fear of alerting predators to the location of their nest. In the first few days of their life, the chicks of many bird species produce feces enclosed in a gelatinous sac. Their parents will swallow this, which suggests that the poop may retain some nutri-

a great **number** of animal species regularly **eat** their own **poop**

tional value that the chick's undeveloped stomach was unable to process. As the chick gets older, the parent bird will stop eating its feces and instead carry them away to be dumped.

Acknowledgments

We would like to thank our wonderful, dedicated literary agent, Andrew Lownie, for making this book happen. We also thank our editor, Andrew John, for professionalism and attention to detail that have gone a long way to covering up our own deficiencies in these areas. Many thanks to Claudia Dyer and Helen Stanton at Piatkus and Sara Carder, Andrew Yackira, and all the team at Tarcher. Finally, we thank our families for their continuing patience, support, and encouragement.

For more kid-tastic facts, look for

Why Fish Fart

Gross but True Things

You'll Wish You Didn't Know